200
Soups

Madge Baird

GIBBS SMITH
TO ENRICH AND INSPIRE HUMANKIND

Heartfelt appreciation for taste testing and encouragement goes to: Veldon and Karen; Carl and Kathryn; Suzanne and Dee; Patty, Boyd and McKay; Florene; Katherine and Phyllis; the Sullivans; the Ukenas; Melissa, Renee, and Anita; the Petersons; Pixie, Glennis, Stacy W., Maryanne, Lei Lani, Stacy S., Marci, and all the ladies of FHE. Special thanks to Suzanne P., Cathy, Marilyn, Kay, Stacy A., Keri, Lanette, and my editor, Michelle, for sharing family-favorite recipes and for tossing ideas for new combinations my way. Soup's on!

First Edition
15 14 13 12   5 4 3 2

Text © 2011 Madge Baird

Published by
Gibbs Smith
P.O. Box 667
Layton, Utah 84041

1.800.835.4993 orders
www.gibbs-smith.com

Designed by Debra McQuiston
Printed and bound in China

Gibbs Smith books are printed on either recycled, 100% post-consumer waste, FSC-certified papers or on paper produced from a 100% certified sustainable forest/controlled wood source.

Library of Congress Cataloging-in-Publication Data

Baird, Madge.
  200 soups / Madge Baird. — 1st ed.
      p. cm.
  Includes index.
  ISBN 978-1-4236-2331-1
1. Soups. I. Title. II. Title: Two hundred soups.
  TX757.B36 2011
  641.8'13—dc22

                              2011013851

Contents

Helpful
Hints

1. Cooking soup is a creative activity. Enjoy the process.

2. Your own palate is your best guide for how the soup should taste. Taste soups during cooking and adjust.

3. Measurements and ingredients need not be exact. You can increase or decrease amounts of most ingredients and make substitutions.

4. Cooking times are approximate and can often be shortened or extended for your schedule.

5. The base, or flavor foundation, of your soup makes all the difference in its appeal. Keep a variety of broths and bouillons on hand.

6. Other ingredients that deepen a soup's flavor with small additions are tomato paste, and Worcestershire, soy, and Asian fish sauces.

7. Experiment with different thickeners: roux, white sauce, cornstarch, cream of wheat, pureed vegetables, instant potatoes, cream, coconut milk, and more.

8. All references to olive oil here mean extra virgin, but you can choose other grades.

9. Fresh, frozen, and canned vegetables, especially home-canned from the garden, can be used interchangeably.

10. All kinds of tomato products can be used in soups that call for tomatoes, including spaghetti sauce and ketchup.

11. Save little bits of leftover meat or vegetables in separate freezer containers until you need them for a soup.

12. For pureeing, use whatever equipment you have: blender, food processor, smoothie maker, hand-held blender, even a hand-held mixer will work to some degree.

13. The {V} symbol by a recipe title indicates it is vegetarian. Other recipes can become vegetarian with small changes.

14. Soup is meant to be shared. Take some to a neighbor and get something going!

Pureed & Cream Soups

African Peanut Soup {V}

Makes 12–15 *servings*

3 tablespoons peanut or
    vegetable oil
2 cups chopped onion
2 teaspoons red chile
    flakes
2 pounds carrots, peeled
    and cut into 4 pieces
2 large sweet potatoes
    (about 2 pounds),
    peeled and cubed
2 (14-ounce) cans
    vegetable broth
4 cups tomato juice
2 tablespoons grated
    fresh gingerroot
1 1/2 cups peanut butter,
    creamy or chunky
Hot sauce
Chopped peanuts,
    optional

Heat oil in a large soup pot over medium-high heat. Saute onion and chile flakes until onion becomes translucent. Add carrots, sweet potatoes, and broth; add just enough water to cover the vegetables. Cover and bring to a boil; cook until vegetables are tender, about 20–25 minutes. Stir tomato juice and gingerroot into the vegetables. Using a hand-held blender, puree soup to a smooth consistency right in the pot. If you use a stand blender, puree in batches. Heat the puree and stir in peanut butter. Season to taste with hot sauce (should have a mild bite but not sting). Serve hot. Garnish with peanuts, if you wish.

Butternut-Apple Soup

Makes 6–8 servings

4 cups cooked butternut
   squash, mashed*
2 large green apples,
   chopped
1½ cups apple juice or
   cider
2–3 rounded teaspoons
   chicken bouillon
   powder
1 tablespoon dehydrated
   onion flakes
⅛ teaspoon pepper
½ cup fat-free
   half-and-half
Parmesan cheese,
   optional

Spray the bottom of a medium saucepan with nonstick cooking spray. Place all ingredients in the pan, except the half-and-half and cheese, and stir together. Bring soup to a boil over medium-high heat, stirring frequently. Use a splatter guard. When soup is bubbling, reduce heat to low, cover with a lid, and let simmer until apples have softened, about 20 minutes. Stir frequently to avoid sticking. Remove pan from heat, transfer soup to a food processor and puree to desired smoothness. Return puree to pan and stir in half-and-half. Heat over medium-high to the boiling point. Remove from heat and ladle into bowls. Sprinkle lightly with cheese, if desired.

*Start with squash puree if you wish.

Rosemary-Apple Butternut Soup

Makes 4–6 *servings*

**1 tart apple, peeled and
   chopped**
¹/₂ small onion, chopped
3 tablespoons butter
**1 Knorr chicken
   bouillon cube**
3 cups water
**¹/₂ teaspoon chopped
   fresh rosemary**
1 slice wheat bread
**¹/₂ large butternut
   squash, baked and
   peeled**
¹/₂ cup whipping cream
Salt and pepper

In a medium saucepan, saute apple and onion in butter for 4-5 minutes, stirring frequently. Add all remaining ingredients, except cream and salt and pepper. Bring to a low boil for 15 minutes. Remove from heat and let cool a little, then transfer to a food processor. Add cream and process until smooth. Return to saucepan and heat. Add salt and pepper, to taste.

Gingered Apple-Pumpkin Soup

Makes 10–12 servings

2 tablespoons olive oil
1 large onion, chopped
2 stalks celery, chopped
1/2 pound of bacon,
    chopped
1 (15-ounce) can
    pumpkin
1 cup water
2 cups apple cider
1/4 cup brown sugar
1/2 teaspoon Chinese
    five-spice powder
4 cubes chicken bouillon
1 unpeeled apple,
    chopped
Dash liquid smoke
Salt and pepper
1 tablespoon grated
    fresh gingerroot,
    not packed
Sour cream, optional

Heat oil in a large heavy-bottomed soup pot. Lightly saute onion, celery, and bacon. Add pumpkin, water, apple cider, brown sugar, five-spice, bouillon, apple, liquid smoke, salt, pepper, and gingerroot to the pot. Cover and simmer for 35–40 minutes, stirring frequently. Puree in batches until smooth. Serve with a dollop of sour cream, if you wish.

Gingered Carrot and Sweet Potato Soup

Makes 8–10 servings

½ cup diced onion
½ cup diced celery
1 tablespoon olive oil
1 tablespoon butter
1 pound carrots, cut in rounds
2 cups diced sweet potato
1 (14.5-ounce) can chicken broth
2 cups water
2 cubes chicken bouillon
1 teaspoon nutmeg
1½ cups whipping cream
Salt

In a large saucepan, saute onion and celery in oil and butter until onion turns translucent. Add carrots, sweet potato, broth, and water and bring to a gentle boil. Cover and simmer for 15–20 minutes, until vegetables are tender. Puree vegetables in their liquid until smooth, using either a hand-held or stand blender. Heat again, adding nutmeg, cream, and a sprinkle of salt. Taste and adjust seasonings.

Whippy Carrot and Parsnip Bisque

Makes 4–6 *servings*

6–8 whole carrots,
    peeled and sliced
4–6 parsnips, peeled
    and sliced
¼ cup diced onion
1½ cups water
1½ teaspoons chicken
    bouillon powder
Zest and segmented
    fruit of 1 orange
1 cup whipping cream
¼ teaspoon mace
¼ teaspoon nutmeg
1 teaspoon salt

In a medium saucepan, boil carrots, parsnips, and onion in water until tender. Begin pureeing vegetables and the cooking water together. When vegetables are broken down, add all remaining ingredients. Puree until smooth using either a hand-held or stand blender.

Carrot Velvet Soup

Makes 6–8 servings

4 large carrots, sliced
1/2 teaspoon ground cloves
1/4 teaspoon coriander seed, smashed, optional
2 1/2 cups chicken broth
2 teaspoons sugar
1 cup half-and-half
Pepper
Chives

In a large saucepan, boil the first five ingredients together until carrots are very tender, about 25 minutes. Puree with a hand-held blender until smooth, add half-and-half, and heat, stirring frequently. Season with pepper, to taste. If you use a stand blender, puree in batches and return puree to pan before adding half-and-half. Serve hot or at room temperature, with chives for garnish.

Lemon-Thyme Green Bean Soup {V}

Makes 6 servings

1 1/2 pounds fresh green beans
1 1/2 cups water
2/3 cup butter
1/2 cup flour
1/4 teaspoon dried thyme
6 cups milk
2 cubes vegetable bouillon
Salt and pepper
2 teaspoons lemon juice

Steam beans in a medium covered saucepan for about 6–7 minutes. Drain and quickly plunge into cold water; drain when cool.

In the same saucepan, melt butter and stir in flour and thyme; cook for 2 minutes. Slowly add milk, whisking constantly until it thickens; remove from heat. Puree beans, white sauce, and bouillon together in batches. Reheat puree, season with salt, pepper, and lemon juice.

Lemony Asparagus Soup {V}

Makes 4 small servings

1 cup water
1 pound asparagus,
    cleaned and woody
    stems snapped off
1 cube vegetable
    bouillon
Pinch garlic powder
2 teaspoons lemon zest
1/2 cup whipping cream

Bring water to a boil in a medium saucepan and add asparagus, snapping into smaller pieces as you go. Add bouillon, garlic powder, and zest. Cover pan and steam asparagus for 4 minutes, until just tender and still brightly colored. Remove from heat and puree asparagus with its liquid until smooth. Add cream and puree until well blended. Taste and adjust seasonings. Serve hot or cold.

Creamy Tomato Soup {V}

Makes 4 servings

1/2 cup chopped onion
2 tablespoons olive oil
2 tablespoons flour
1 pound tomatoes,
    peeled and chopped,
    or 2 (14.5-ounce)
    cans tomatoes, whole
    or diced, with liquid
1 cup whipping cream

In a medium saucepan over medium heat, saute onion in oil until it turns translucent. Add flour to the onion and cook for 1 minute. Whisk the tomatoes into the onion mixture. If using fresh, simmer for 3 minutes; if using canned, proceed with the cream. To prevent cream from curdling, stir about 1/2 cup tomatoes into the cream before stirring the remaining cream into the soup.

Creamy Fresh Tomato Soup {V}

Makes 4 servings

1/2 cup chopped onion
1 tablespoon olive oil
1 pound tomatoes, peeled, seeded, and roughly chopped
1/2 cup roughly chopped basil leaves
1 1/2 teaspoons salt
1/4 teaspoon pepper
6 ounces herb and garlic cream cheese spread

In a medium saucepan, saute onion in oil over medium heat for 4 minutes; do not let burn. Add all remaining ingredients except cream cheese. Cover pan and cook on a low boil for 5–8 minutes, stirring frequently. Puree until smooth. Return soup to heat and stir in cream cheese until melted. Taste and adjust seasonings.

Broccoli Slaw Soup

Makes 4 servings

1 (12-ounce) package broccoli slaw
1 (14.5-ounce) can chicken broth
1 cup water
1 teaspoon chicken bouillon powder
1 teaspoon lemon zest
1/2 teaspoon oregano
1 cup half-and-half
4–6 tablespoons cream of wheat
Pepper

In a medium saucepan, bring all ingredients except half-and half and cream of wheat to a boil. Reduce heat and simmer for 5 minutes, or until broccoli is just cooked. Remove from heat and puree the soup until smooth, then reheat. In a separate small saucepan, heat half-and-half and stir in cream of wheat to make a sauce. Incorporate sauce into the soup.

Tomatillo-Avocado Soup

Makes 6–8 small servings

1 small onion, roughly chopped
1 clove garlic, minced
1 tablespoon vegetable oil
1 pound fresh tomatillos,* husks removed and roughly chopped
1 (14.5-ounce) can chicken broth
1 teaspoon salt
1/2 teaspoon cumin
1/4 teaspoon dried Mexican oregano
2 ripe Haas avocadoes, seeded and scooped from skins
1/2 cup fresh cilantro
1 teaspoon sugar
2 teaspoons lime juice
4 tablespoons whipping cream, optional**

In a medium saucepan, saute onion and garlic in oil over medium-high heat for 3 minutes. Do not let burn. Add tomatillos, broth, salt, and spices. Cover pan and let simmer for 7–10 minutes, until tomatillos are soft; remove from heat. Add avocado, cilantro, sugar, and juice. Puree all together until smooth. Taste and adjust seasonings with salt, sugar, or cream. Reheat or serve at room temperature.

*Choose ones that are lighter in color, even yellow. The darkest green tomatillos are underripe for this recipe.

**Cream will help mellow a blend that is too tart for the taste.

Sweet Potato, Pineapple, and Bacon Soup

Makes 4 servings

1/4 small onion, finely chopped
1 tablespoon butter
1 teaspoon bacon grease
2 rounded teaspoons crispy crumbled bacon
1 tablespoon chicken bouillon powder
1/2 cup chunk pineapple, drained
1/4 cup raisins
2 teaspoons tomato paste
1 teaspoon soy sauce
1 jumbo or 2 medium baked sweet potatoes
1/2 cup half-and-half
2 teaspoons cornstarch

In a medium saucepan, saute the onion for 3 minutes in butter and bacon grease. Add all remaining ingredients except half-and-half and cornstarch. Cover and simmer for 10 minutes. Let cool, then transfer to a food processor and add half-and-half and cornstarch. Blend until soup is a smooth consistency. Return to saucepan and heat. Taste and adjust seasoning 1/2 teaspoon at a time with more bouillon, if desired.

Creamy Parsnip and Apple Soup

Makes 4 servings

1 small onion, chopped
2 tablespoons butter
2 tablespoons olive oil
2 tart-sweet apples,
    peeled and chopped
1¼ pounds parsnips,
    peeled and chopped
3 cups water
1 tablespoon chicken
    bouillon powder
1 tablespoon lemon juice
1 teaspoon salt
½ teaspoon cinnamon
½ teaspoon nutmeg
1 cup whipping cream
1 cup milk
1 tablespoon cornstarch
    mixed with 2
    tablespoons water,
    optional

In a large saucepan, saute onion in butter and oil over medium heat for 3 minutes. Add apples and saute 3–4 minutes more. Add parsnips, water, flavorings, and spices. Cover and bring to a boil; reduce heat and simmer for 20 minutes, until parsnips are tender. Let cool a little, then puree the soup and return to pan, adding cream and milk. Heat to just boiling, stirring frequently. If soup is too thin, thicken with cornstarch mixture.

VARIATION: You can convert this recipe to vegetarian by substituting vegetable bouillon powder and reducing onion to ½ cup.

Spring Pea Soup

Makes 8–10 *servings*

2 tablespoons olive oil
1 tablespoon butter
1/3 cup finely chopped
    onion
1/3 cup finely chopped
    leek (tender green
    part included)
2 medium russet
    potatoes, finely diced
2 (14.5-ounce) cans
    chicken broth
1 pound freshly shelled
    or frozen peas
1 teaspoon marjoram or
    2 teaspoons freshly
    minced mint
Water
2 teaspoons chicken
    bouillon powder,
    optional
Pepper
2 egg yolks
1 1/2 cups whipping cream
Sour cream, optional
Freshly snipped chives,
    optional

In a large saucepan, heat oil and butter over medium heat. Saute onion and leek, stirring frequently, for about 7 minutes, until onion turns translucent. Add potatoes and broth. Cover and bring to a boil, then reduce heat and let simmer for 10–12 minutes. Add peas, herb, and 1–2 cups water, if needed, to cover. Bring to a low boil again and let cook for 6–7 minutes, until peas are cooked but still bright green. Remove from heat and let cool slightly. Puree mixture until smooth. Taste and adjust flavor with bouillon and pepper, if desired.

In a small bowl, whisk egg yolks thoroughly, then add cream and whisk together. Temper the cream mixture with 1/2 cup puree, then a second 1/2 cup. Pour all the cream mixture into the puree and stir well. Reheat and serve. Garnish with a dollop of sour cream or chives.

Cream of Zucchini Soup

2 pounds zucchini or
    1 very large zucchini
1 tablespoon dehydrated
    onion flakes
1½ cups water
1 teaspoon seasoned salt
1 teaspoon dill weed
1 tablespoon or 3 cubes
    chicken bouillon
1½ cups milk
6 tablespoons butter
5–6 tablespoons flour
Pepper

Trim ends from zucchini and cut into thick rounds. Place zucchini and onion in a medium saucepan with water, cover pan, and boil until zucchini is tender. Puree zucchini and liquid in a blender until it is fully liquefied (green flecks will be visible). Return puree to the saucepan and add salt, dill, bouillon, and milk. Reheat on medium heat, stirring frequently.

In a medium frying pan, make roux by melting butter and stirring in flour; cook about 3 minutes, stirring and mashing so all the flour gets cooked. Ladle soup into the roux in small portions and stir together; little by little the roux will absorb the liquid and become creamy. When it is creamy enough to pour or spoon into the saucepan, do so; whisk roux into soup vigorously to prevent flour lumps. Taste soup and adjust seasoning with pepper and a small amount of bouillon, if needed.

Parmesan-Spinach Soup

Makes 4–6 *servings*

1 (10-ounce) package
   fresh or frozen
   spinach
2 teaspoons dehydrated
   onion flakes
2 teaspoons chicken
   bouillon
Pinch garlic powder
2 cups water
4 tablespoons butter
5 tablespoons flour
1 cup milk
3 tablespoons grated
   Parmesan cheese
1/4 cup whipping cream

Place spinach, onion, bouillon, and garlic powder in a medium saucepan and cover with the water. Place a lid on the pan and bring to a boil for about 2–3 minutes. Remove from heat and puree the spinach and liquid. Return puree to the saucepan and reheat.

Meanwhile, make a cream sauce: melt the butter in a small saucepan then stir in the flour and let cook for 3 minutes, stirring frequently. Pour in the milk 1/4 cup at a time, whisking the milk into the flour until creamy, then add more milk and repeat the process until all the milk has been added. Whisk the cheese into the milk, then pour the milk into the soup and whisk together. Heat on medium high until the soup boils then remove from the heat. Add cream and stir. Taste and adjust seasonings.

Cream of Leafy Green Soup

Makes 8 servings

1 leek, green part only, thinly sliced
1/2 cup chopped onion
2 tablespoons olive oil
1 small zucchini, sliced
2 bunches leafy greens (kale, collards, mustard, chard), tough stems discarded
3 cups water
1 tablespoon chicken or vegetable bouillon powder
1 large handful baby spinach
3 tablespoons butter
3 tablespoons flour
1 cup whipping cream
Pepper

In a large saucepan, saute the leek and onion in oil for 4–5 minutes. Add zucchini, greens, water, and bouillon to the pan. Cover and boil just until greens are tender, about 8 minutes. Remove from heat. Add spinach to the pan and push under the water. Let sit 5 minutes. Puree greens with their liquid.

Make a roux of the butter and flour, cooking about 3 minutes. Thin/temper the roux by adding puree to the flour mixture in small increments until the roux is thin enough to spoon into the soup. Return puree and roux to the pan and whisk together; reheat. Stir in cream. Taste and season with pepper.

Cream of Broccoli Soup

Makes 6 servings

1 large bunch broccoli, stems and florets cut into pieces
1 tablespoon dehydrated onion flakes
2 (14.5-ounce) cans chicken broth
1 cup water
2 tablespoons butter
2 tablespoons flour
1 cup milk
1 cup whipping cream

In a covered medium saucepan, steam broccoli and onion in the broth and water until fork-tender, about 10 minutes. Puree broccoli and liquid in batches in a blender or a food processor to desired consistency.

In a large saucepan, melt butter and stir in flour. Pour in milk, stirring constantly. Add broccoli puree to the milk then stir in the cream. Stir constantly while heating through.

Creamy Cauliflower Soup

Makes 4–6 servings

1 small head cauliflower, cleaned and broken into florets
$1^{1}/_2$ cups water
2 teaspoons chicken bouillon
$^{1}/_4$ teaspoon nutmeg
1 tablespoon butter
$^{1}/_4$ cup whipping cream
$^{3}/_4$ cup milk, divided
Pepper

Place the cauliflower and water in a medium saucepan; cover and bring to a boil, cooking until a fork inserts easily into a thicker piece of cauliflower. Remove from heat and add all remaining ingredients except for $^{1}/_4$ cup of the milk. Let cool slightly, then puree in batches in a stand blender or with a hand-held blender until smooth. If it seems too thick, add the remaining milk. Season with pepper, if you wish.

Roasted Red Pepper Soup {V}

Makes 4 servings

3 red bell peppers, roasted and skin removed*
6 ripe plum tomatoes, quartered
1/2 cup water
2 tablespoons lemon juice
1/2 cube Knorr vegetable bouillon
Pinch red chile flakes
Pinch pepper
1/2 cup whipping cream

Place all ingredients except cream in a medium saucepan and bring to a boil, stirring. Reduce heat to a simmer and cook for 3–4 minutes while tomatoes break down. Transfer tomato mixture to a blender or food processor and puree. Return to the saucepan and add cream; heat through.

*Roast peppers over the flame of a gas stove, on the grill, or under the broiler until the skin is charred all over. Let cool wrapped in wet paper towels or in a sealed plastic bag. When cool, remove stems and seeds, then gently scrape off the charred skin with a spoon.

Vegetable Soups

Sweet Ham and Vegetable Soup

Makes 10–12 servings

2–3 tablespoons olive oil

1 large onion, chopped

4 ribs celery, chopped

6 carrots, peeled and chopped

2 pounds red potatoes, peeled and diced

3 cups diced cooked ham

1 bay leaf

1½ teaspoons oregano

1 teaspoon seasoned salt

6 cups water

3 (14-ounce) cans chicken broth

1 (15-ounce) can green beans, drained

1 (15-ounce) can red kidney beans, drained and rinsed

1 (15-ounce) can great Northern white beans, drained and rinsed

1 quart or 2 (15-ounce) cans crushed or diced tomatoes

1 (6-ounce) can tomato paste

½ cup drippings from glazed ham or 2 tablespoons brown sugar

2 teaspoons Worcestershire sauce

Salt and pepper

In a large soup pot, heat oil over medium-high heat. Saute onion, celery, and carrots together for about 8 minutes while onion turns translucent and vegetables begin to cook. Add potatoes, ham, herbs, seasoned salt, water, and broth. Cover pot and bring to a boil over medium-high heat, stirring occasionally; reduce heat and let simmer for about 30 minutes, until vegetables are tender.

Add all other ingredients except salt and pepper and bring to a boil again; reduce heat and simmer 15 minutes while flavors meld. Adjust seasoning with salt and pepper.

Slow Alphabet Vegetable Soup

Makes about 12 servings

1½ pounds lean beef
   steak such as sirloin,
   cut in cubes
2 tablespoons olive oil
1 medium onion, chopped
2 ribs celery, thinly
   sliced
1 (15-ounce) can corn,
   drained
2 (15-ounce) cans cut
   green beans, drained
5 medium carrots,
   peeled and sliced
1 (6-ounce) can tomato
   paste
1 (14.5-ounce) can beef
   broth
2 teaspoons soy sauce
1 bay leaf
1 teaspoon dried basil
1 cup water
¾ cup alphabet pasta
Salt and pepper

In a large frying pan, brown beef in hot oil on both sides. Place all ingredients, except pasta, salt, and pepper, in a 5-quart slow cooker. Add water to cover vegetables. Cover and cook on low for 6–8 hours, until vegetables are tender. Add pasta and stir into the liquid. Cover again and turn heat to high for about 30 minutes, until pasta has swelled to more than double its size. Season to taste with salt and pepper.

If you have leftover soup, the pasta will likely continue to absorb the liquid; you'll need to add about 1 cup of water or beef broth when you serve it again.

Wild Rice and Mushroom Soup

Makes 6–8 *servings*

- 1 cup uncooked white, brown, and wild rice blend
- 2 teaspoons salt
- 2 cups cold water
- 2 slices bacon, chopped
- 2 tablespoons olive oil
- 4 tablespoons unsalted butter, divided
- 8–10 ounces baby portabella mushrooms, sliced
- 1 leek, chopped, white and tender green parts
- 3 tablespoons flour
- 2 (14.5-ounce) cans chicken broth
- Juice of 1/2 lemon
- 1 cup half-and-half
- 1/4 cup whipping cream
- 1 tablespoon chopped flat-leaf parsley
- 1/2 teaspoon pepper
- 1 teaspoon salt

Cook rice in salted water according to package directions.

Cook bacon in a large frying pan over medium-high heat until it renders some of its fat. Add oil plus 2 tablespoons butter and let heat. Add mushrooms and saute with the bacon until mushrooms begin to brown. Transfer mushrooms and bacon to a cutting board, reserving liquid in the pan, and let cool. Chop the mushrooms and reserve with bacon.

Add remaining 2 tablespoons butter and leek to the pan. Saute over medium heat for 3–4 minutes, until it wilts. Return mushroom-bacon mixture to pan and sprinkle all with flour. Toss and cook about 2 minutes. Add mushroom-leek mixture to rice then pour in chicken broth. Deglaze the frying pan with lemon juice then pour that into the rice. Add remaining ingredients and bring to a boil. Taste and adjust salt, if needed.

Cream of Dilly Mushroom Soup {V}

Makes 4 servings

2 tablespoons olive oil
1 tablespoon butter
1 medium onion, chopped
8 ounces white
    mushrooms, sliced
2 teaspoons dill weed
1 (14.5-ounce) can
    vegetable broth
2 tablespoons sour cream
$1/2$ teaspoon paprika
1 teaspoon seasoned salt
4 tablespoons flour
1 cup milk
3 ounces plain yogurt
Salt and pepper

In a medium saucepan, heat oil and butter. Saute onion on medium-high heat until it begins to turn translucent. Add mushrooms and continue cooking until they have turned glossy and slightly brown. Sprinkle with dill weed and cook 1 minute longer. Stir in broth, sour cream, paprika, and seasoned salt. Bring to a boil.

Whisk flour into the milk. Add milk and yogurt to the saucepan and bring to a boil over medium-high heat, stirring, until soup thickens. Taste and adjust flavor with salt and pepper, if desired.

Stone Soup*

Makes 8–10 servings

4–5 cups chopped
vegetables (fresh,
canned and drained,
frozen, or leftover)
1 cup dry starch product
or 2–3 cups cooked
(instant rice, pasta,
quick-cooking
barley, or quinoa)
1 tablespoon dehydrated
onion flakes
6–8 cups water
1–2 cups cooked meat or
poultry, optional
4 teaspoons or cubes
bouillon (beef or
chicken)
2 cups liquid tomato
(diced, stewed, sauce,
juice, spaghetti
sauce, canned soup)
2 teaspoons cumin
1 teaspoon dried oregano
1 teaspoon dried basil
Salt and pepper

Place all raw vegetables and
uncooked starch ingredients in
a large soup pot with the onion
and water. Bring to a low boil
and cook for 5 minutes. Add all
remaining ingredients; cover pot
and simmer soup for 15–20 minutes. Add more liquid, if needed.
Taste and adjust seasonings with
small additions of tomato or
bouillon, plus salt and pepper.

*You can find the story of stone
soup on Wikipedia. Tell it to your
family and then send them on a
treasure hunt in your refrigerator
and pantry to gather ingredients.

Winter Vegetable Soup {V}

Makes 8 servings

4 medium potatoes,
   peeled and cubed
2 medium turnips,
   peeled and cubed
1 medium onion, diced
2 ribs celery, sliced
$1/3$ cup diced green bell
   pepper
3 cups sliced cabbage
4–5 cups water
1 (8-ounce) can tomato
   sauce
2 tablespoons prepared
   chili sauce
1 tablespoon vegetable
   bouillon powder
$1/2$ teaspoon basil
$1/2$ teaspoon oregano
Salt and pepper

Place vegetables and water in a large saucepan, cover, and boil until tender, about 20 minutes. Add the tomato sauce, chili sauce, bouillon, and seasonings; stir. Simmer 10 minutes more. Taste and adjust seasonings.

Russian-Style Cabbage Soup

Makes 8 servings

1 medium onion, diced
2 ribs celery, diced
4 whole carrots, chopped
2 tablespoon olive oil
3 medium russet
   potatoes, scrubbed
   and cubed
4 cups shredded
   cabbage
2 (15-ounce) cans diced
   tomatoes, with liquid
2 (14.5-ounce) cans
   chicken broth
4 cups water
1 bay leaf
1/2 teaspoon pepper
Salt

In a large soup pot, saute onion, celery, and carrot in oil for 5–7 minutes, until onion begins to turn translucent. Add all remaining ingredients; cover pot and simmer soup for 40–60 minutes. Add more water during cooking, if needed, to keep the vegetables covered. Taste and adjust seasonings.

Beet and Apple Soup {V}

Makes 6–8 small servings

1 tablespoon olive oil
1 teaspoon butter
2 red cooking apples, peeled and thinly sliced
1 carrot, peeled and thinly sliced
1 stalk celery, thinly sliced
2 (14-ounce) cans beets, drained
1 cup apple juice
1 (14.5-ounce) can vegetable broth
1 bay leaf
$1/2$ teaspoon salt
$1/4$ teaspoon pepper
Vegetable bouillon powder
$1/4$ cup whipping cream, optional

Heat oil and butter in a medium saucepan. Place apples, carrot, and celery in pan and saute, covered, until softened. Add beets, apple juice, broth, bay leaf, salt, and pepper to the pan. Bring to a low boil and cook, covered, about 20 minutes, while bay leaf infuses the broth; discard bay leaf. Puree soup until smooth then heat through and taste; adjust seasoning with $1/2$ teaspoon bouillon powder, if desired. Cream can be added to mellow the flavor.

Harvest Moon Soup

Makes 8 servings

1 onion, chopped
2–3 cloves garlic, minced
2 tablespoons olive oil
2 tablespoons butter
1 cup chopped fresh
    herbs (basil, oregano,
    dill, rosemary, mint)
1 bay leaf
8 cups chopped fresh
    vegetables (tomatoes,
    corn, summer squash,
    turnips, carrots,
    peppers, broccoli,
    cabbage, greens)
3 cups chicken broth*
3 cups vegetable broth*
Salt and pepper
Parmesan cheese

In a large soup pot, saute onion and garlic in oil and butter for 4–5 minutes. Add fresh herbs and saute for 1 minute more. Add bay leaf, all vegetables, and liquids. Cover pot and bring soup to a boil; cook for 20–25 minutes, until vegetables are fork-tender. Taste and adjust seasonings with salt and pepper. Serve garnished with cheese, if desired.

*Can substitute 6 cups water plus 6 small or 3 large chicken or vegetable bouillon cubes.

Yellow Summer Soup

Makes 4–6 *servings*

6 ears fresh corn or 12 ounces frozen corn kernels

3 green onions, thinly sliced, white and green parts

2–3 yellow summer squash, diced

1 yellow bell pepper, diced

2 tablespoons olive oil

2 tablespoons butter

2 (14-ounce) cans chicken broth

Salt and pepper

Cilantro

In a large soup pot, boil the ears of corn about 3 minutes then remove from water to cool. When cool, cut corn from the cob and set aside.

In a medium saucepan over medium-high heat, saute onion, squash, and bell pepper in hot oil and butter just until the vegetables heat through, about 4 minutes. Stir frequently. Add corn and broth to the squash-bell pepper mixture and heat until the liquid begins to boil. Remove from heat. Adjust seasonings with salt and pepper. Garnish each bowl of soup with fresh cilantro.

Italian Garden Vegetable Soup {V}

Makes 6–8 *servings*

2 medium zucchini, sliced

2 medium yellow summer squash, sliced

1 small or medium eggplant, diced

6 medium tomatoes, diced

2–4 ears corn, kernels cut off the cob

1 clove garlic, minced

1 (14.5-ounce) can vegetable broth

$1/2$ cup chopped fresh basil

$1/4$ cup chopped fresh parsley

$1/4$–$1/2$ teaspoon onion salt

Salt and pepper

Place all ingredients in a large saucepan. Bring to a boil and then reduce heat to steam vegetables in broth for 10 minutes. Adjust seasonings with salt and pepper.

Vegetarian Minestrone {V}

Makes 4–5 quarts

1 medium onion, chopped
1 cup sliced celery
2 tablespoons vegetable
    oil
3 cups thinly sliced
    cabbage
3 cups hot water
1 cup chopped fresh
    basil, oregano and
    thyme or 1 tablespoon
    plus 1 teaspoon dried
    herbs
1/2 teaspoon garlic
    powder
2 cups sliced carrots
2 cups cut green beans
2 cups broccoli florets
2 small zucchini, halved
    and sliced
1 yellow summer squash,
    halved and sliced
2 large handfuls spinach
    leaves
6 cups diced tomatoes
Water
Salt and pepper
1 pound shell or tube
    pasta, optional

In a large soup pot, saute onion and celery in oil. Add cabbage and hot water. Cover with a lid, raise heat to medium high and bring to a boil. Cook about 10 minutes to let cabbage soften then continue adding herbs, garlic powder, and other vegetables, longest-cooking ones first. Add enough water to cover vegetables. When all vegetables have been added, pour in the tomatoes and continue boiling lightly for about 15 minutes while the vegetables flavor the broth. Season with salt and pepper.

Add pasta at this point, if using. Be sure there is enough water to cook the pasta. When pasta is cooked, taste and adjust seasonings with salt, pepper, and more herbs.

Beefy Wheat Berry Soup

Makes 4 servings

3 large potatoes, peeled and diced

2 tablespoons olive oil

2 carrots, sliced

1 (14.5-ounce) can cut green beans, drained

1 cup diced turnip

1 cup frozen corn

1 cup cooked wheat berries*

1 (1.3-ounce) envelope onion soup and dip mix

2 Knorr beef bouillon cubes

1 tablespoon tomato paste

1 teaspoon sugar

4 cups water

1 tablespoon cider vinegar

Preheat oven to 450 degrees.

Toss potatoes in oil then spread in a single layer on a baking sheet. Bake for 20 minutes; remove from oven and place potatoes in a large saucepan with all remaining ingredients. Cover and bring to a boil; reduce heat and simmer for 30–40 minutes.

*Simmer 1 cup hard winter wheat in 3 cups lightly salted water, uncovered, 45 minutes to 1 hour. Use the excess as cereal or add to a salad.

Creamy Cheddar Vegetable Soup {V}

Makes 4–6 *servings*

1 pound frozen mixed
   vegetables (broccoli,
   carrots, cauliflower,
   onions, snow peas)
1 (14.5-ounce) can
   vegetable broth
1 cup water
1 cup Wacky Mac pasta
2 tablespoons butter
2 tablespoons flour
1 cup milk
1½ cups grated cheddar
   cheese
Pepper

Cut larger vegetables into smaller pieces. In a medium covered saucepan, steam vegetables in broth and water for 15 minutes. Add pasta and cook 8–10 minutes more.

Meanwhile, make the white sauce in a small saucepan by cooking the butter and flour together for 3–4 minutes, stirring frequently. Then whisk in the milk until smooth. Add cheese to sauce and stir until melted. Pour sauce into the vegetables and liquid; stir well to blend. Simmer for 2–3 minutes while the broth thickens. Season to taste with pepper.

So Easy Chicken-Broccoli Soup with Cheese

Makes 4 servings

2 heads broccoli with stems
3/4 cup water
6 slices medium or sharp cheddar cheese
2 (10.5-ounce) cans cream of chicken soup, condensed
2/3 cup milk
1 1/2 cups cut-up rotisserie chicken
1/2 teaspoon pepper

Cut away about half of the broccoli stem and discard. Peel the remaining stem with a vegetable peeler then cut it off the head and slice the stem into thin rings. Cut the head into florets. Bring broccoli and water to a boil in a medium covered saucepan over medium-high heat. Reduce heat to medium and let broccoli steam for 3–4 minutes, until fork-tender. Remove from heat.

Break cheese slices into smaller pieces, add to broccoli, and fold in. Add all remaining ingredients and stir to combine. Return to stove over medium heat; stir frequently to avoid scorching while soup heats and cheese melts.

Peas and Carrots
Cheez Whiz Soup

Makes 10–12 *servings*

3 sticks butter
1½ cups flour
1 (16-ounce) jar Cheez
  Whiz
3 quarts water
1 large onion, diced
2 ribs celery, diced
¼ cup chicken base*
16 ounces frozen peas
  and carrots

In a medium frying pan, melt butter and stir in flour to make roux. Cook over medium heat, stirring frequently, until flour is cooked and just begins to turn golden, about 5 minutes. Remove from heat and set aside.

Meanwhile, melt Cheez Whiz in a microwave until soft.

In a large soup pot, bring water to a boil and add onion and celery; cover and let boil 3–4 minutes. Add chicken base and roux to water and stir until creamy. Add peas and carrots and let simmer 15 minutes. Remove from heat, add melted Cheez Whiz, and stir again until creamy.

*If you cannot find chicken base, make your own by dissolving 8 bouillon cubes in ¼ cup boiling water.

Creamy Corn and Roasted Poblano Soup

Makes 4 servings

1 tablespoon vegetable
  oil
1 tablespoon butter
1 small onion, diced
1/2 red bell pepper,
  chopped
1 clove garlic, minced
1 (12-ounce) package
  frozen corn
1 (14.5-ounce) can corn,
  with liquid
2 poblano chiles,
  roasted* and diced
1 (14.5-ounce) can
  chicken broth
4 ounces cream cheese
1 cup half-and-half
1/2 cup chopped fresh
  cilantro
Salt and pepper
1 scallion, green part
  only, chopped

In a medium saucepan, heat oil and butter. Saute onion, bell pepper, and garlic over medium heat for 5–7 minutes, until onion turns translucent. Add corn, chiles, and broth, and bring to a boil. Remove from heat and puree a third to a half of the soup, reserving the rest. Add the puree back into the soup along with the cream cheese, half-and-half, and cilantro. Reheat. When hot, taste and adjust seasonings with salt and pepper. Serve with a garnish of scallion.

*See page 25 for roasting instructions.

Basic Fresh Tomato Soup

Makes 6–8 *servings*

**2 pounds ripe tomatoes
(any red, yellow, or
orange varieties)
1 tablespoon olive oil
3/4 cup chopped onion
1/2 cup chicken broth
1 pinch garlic powder
1/2 teaspoon sugar
Salt
Freshly snipped chives**

Immerse washed tomatoes in a medium soup pot of boiling water for 45–60 seconds, until the skins start to split. Transfer tomatoes to a colander and discard the hot water.

While tomatoes are cooling, rinse the pot thoroughly and return to the stove; add oil and heat on medium-high. Saute the onion until it turns translucent. Remove pot from the heat.

Remove the skins, cores, and as many seeds as possible from the tomatoes. Crush tomatoes with your hands over the soup pot and add them to the onion. Add broth, garlic powder, and sugar. Bring to a slow boil over medium heat, stirring frequently. Simmer soup 5–8 minutes, taste and adjust with salt then remove from heat. Serve the soup as is or puree it. Garnish with chives.

Tomato and Shells Soup {V}

Makes 8 servings

1 large onion, diced
16 ounces shell macaroni
1 quart tomato juice
1 quart stewed tomatoes
2 cups water
Salt and pepper

Place all ingredients in a medium-size soup pot and bring to a boil over medium-high heat. Reduce heat and simmer for 12–15 minutes, until macaroni is soft and expanded. The onion will still be slightly crunchy.

Zucchini and Stewed Tomato Soup {V}

Makes 4 servings

2 (14.5-ounce) cans stewed tomatoes
3 small zucchini, thickly sliced
1 teaspoon sugar
Salt and pepper

Bring tomatoes to a low boil in a medium saucepan. Add zucchini and sugar and bring to a boil again. Reduce heat and simmer 4–5 minutes, until zucchini is tender. Season with salt and pepper.

Fresh Tomato-Pesto Soup

Makes 6–8 *servings*

3 cups basil leaves,
    loosely packed
2 cloves garlic, smashed
    and minced
1/3 cup walnut or pecan
    halves
1 tablespoon lemon juice
1/3 cup Parmesan cheese
4–6 tablespoons olive
    oil, divided
2 pounds red-ripe
    tomatoes, peeled,
    cored, and half the
    seeds removed
1/2 cup chicken broth
Pepper

To make pesto,* place the first five ingredients in a food processor and pulse a few times to chop the basil. With the motor running, pour in most of the olive oil and continue processing until a paste forms. Add the rest of the oil if you want the pesto to be thinner.

Chop the tomatoes and place in a large saucepan with the broth. Bring to a low boil over medium-high heat, stirring frequently. Cook for 5–8 minutes, until tomatoes are heated through. Spoon the pesto into the tomatoes 1 tablespoon at a time according to your taste. Season with pepper.

*Any pesto not used in the soup can be frozen for later use.

Orange and Tomato Soup {V}

Makes 4 servings

1 tablespoon olive oil
1 tablespoon butter
1 medium leek, finely diced
2 (15-ounce) cans crushed tomatoes
Juice and flesh of two oranges, zest reserved
1 teaspoon salt
2 teaspoons sugar
1/4 teaspoon ground cloves
1/2 cup sour cream, divided

In a medium saucepan, heat oil and butter on medium heat and saute leek until it becomes limp. Do not let edges brown. Chop tomatoes and add to the saucepan to simmer on medium-low for 7–8 minutes. Puree the tomatoes and all remaining ingredients together except 1/4 cup sour cream and orange zest. Serve soup warm or chilled, with a dollop of sour cream and a small sprinkling of zest for each serving.

Easy Cream of Tomato Soup

Makes 4 *servings*

2 (15-ounce) cans
   diced Italian-style
   tomatoes
1 clove garlic, smashed
   and minced
2 teaspoons chicken
   bouillon powder
1/2 teaspoon dried basil
1 teaspoon salt
4 ounces less-fat cream
   cheese
1–2 tablespoons cream
   of wheat, divided

In a medium saucepan, bring all ingredients except cream cheese and cream of wheat to a low boil over medium heat. Add cream cheese and puree all together. Return pureed mixture to heat and bring to a low simmer. Add cream of wheat 1–2 teaspoons at a time to thicken soup, as desired.

Stuffed Pepper Soup

Makes 6–8 *servings*

4 tablespoons olive oil

1 medium onion, diced

1 clove garlic, minced, optional

1/2 pound Italian ground turkey or pork sausage

2 green bell peppers, seeded and roughly chopped

2 red bell peppers, seeded and roughly chopped

2 (14.5-ounce) cans crushed tomatoes or 4 cups chopped fresh

1 (8-ounce) can tomato sauce

1 cup water

1 1/2 teaspoons Italian seasoning

1/2 teaspoon seasoned salt

1/2 teaspoon paprika, optional

1/2 teaspoon pepper

Salt

2 cups chicken broth

3 cups cooked white or brown rice

In a large saucepan, heat oil over medium heat; saute onion and garlic for 4 minutes, stirring frequently. Remove from pan and set aside. Brown the turkey or sausage. Return onion to the pan and add all remaining ingredients except broth and rice. Cover and bring to a low boil over medium-high heat. Reduce heat and simmer 12–15 minutes, until peppers are tender. Stir in broth and rice. If more liquid is desired, add water a little at a time. Simmer soup, covered, for 5–10 minutes before serving. Adjust salt and other seasonings, to taste.

Roasted Ratatouille Soup {V}

Makes 6–8 *servings*

6 medium red-ripe
   tomatoes
2 medium zucchini
2 Japanese eggplants
2 medium onions
2 bell peppers, any color
2 cloves garlic
4 tablespoons olive oil
Salt and pepper
1/2 cup chopped fresh
   basil or 2 teaspoons
   dried

Preheat oven to 425 degrees.

Cut all vegetables into chunks and place in a large bowl. Slice garlic and then mince; add to vegetable bowl. Pour olive oil over vegetables, season with salt and pepper, and then toss to coat. Transfer vegetables to a roasting pan. Bake, uncovered, for 45 minutes, or until all vegetables are cooked and some have brown edges. Turn vegetables at least twice during cooking time.

Puree vegetables in batches, with a sprinkling of basil, to the degree of smoothness you like. Mix batches together in a large pot and reheat. Serve hot.

Fresh Tomato with Chicken Soup

Makes 6–8 *servings*

3 tablespoons olive oil

1/2 medium yellow onion, thinly sliced

1 large clove garlic, minced

1 small chile pepper* (e.g, Hungarian wax or jalapeno), seeded and finely diced

1 green bell pepper, thinly sliced

2 Japanese eggplants, sliced in thin rounds

1/2 cup chopped fresh herbs (basil, oregano, thyme)

1 cup chicken broth

1 1/2 cups diced rotisserie chicken

2 full cups cherry tomatoes, halved

Salt

1 (8-ounce) can tomato sauce

4 cups hot cooked brown rice

Heat oil over medium-high in a large frying pan. When hot, add onion, garlic, peppers, eggplants, and herbs. Cover, reduce heat to medium, and cook about 15 minutes, turning frequently, until onion and eggplant are soft. Add broth, chicken, tomatoes, and salt. Cover and simmer about 4 minutes, until tomatoes are heated through. Stir in tomato sauce to thicken the broth. Simmer 2–3 minutes more, uncovered. Serve in bowls over rice.

*Or to taste. The heat from the pepper should not overwhelm the flavor of this fresh tomato soup. Alternatively, use about 1 teaspoon Hungarian paprika.

Spanish Rice Soup

Makes 6–8 *servings*

2 tablespoons olive oil
2 tablespoons butter
1 cup uncooked long-
   grain rice
1/2 medium onion, finely
   chopped
1 green or red bell
   pepper, diced
2 teaspoons chicken
   bouillon powder
1 teaspoons seasoned
   salt
1/2 teaspoon sugar
1 (6-ounce) can tomato
   paste
1 (14-ounce) can diced
   tomatoes
4 cups water
Salt and pepper

Heat oil and butter in a large saucepan over medium-high heat; saute rice until it begins to turn golden. Add onion and bell pepper and saute 3–4 more minutes. Add all remaining ingredients and combine well. Cover pan and simmer about 30 minutes, stirring occasionally, until rice grains are soft to the tooth. Taste and adjust seasonings with small additions of bouillon, salt, and pepper.

Red Tomato Gazpacho {V}

Makes 12–15 *servings*

5 pounds tomatoes, peeled
2 cucumbers, peeled and sliced
1 large green bell pepper, seeded and sliced
1 medium red onion, quartered
2 large cloves garlic, minced
1 bunch cilantro, thick stems discarded
$1/4$ cup red wine vinegar
$1/4$ cup olive oil
Juice of 1 lime
32 ounces tomato juice
Salt and pepper
Parmesan cheese
Croutons

Using a food processor, process all vegetable plus garlic in batches to desired consistency. Pour into a large bowl and add remaining ingredients except cheese and croutons. Serve cold in cups or bowls with garnishes.

Cucumber and Green Tomato Gazpacho {V}

Makes 4–6 *servings*

4 medium cucumbers, peeled and roughly chopped

2 medium-size green tomatoes (choose those with a white cast)

1 thick slice purple onion, roughly chopped

1 clove garlic, finely minced

1 green or red bell pepper, seeded and roughly chopped

2 slices soft white bread or 1 slice rustic bread, crusts removed, torn

3 tablespoons extra virgin olive oil

2 teaspoons red wine vinegar

Juice of 1 lime

$1/2$ teaspoon sugar

$1/4$ teaspoon cumin

$1/2$ bunch cilantro, long stems removed

1 teaspoon salt

Croutons

Place all ingredients in the work bowl of a food processor fitted with a metal blade. Pulse a few times to combine and make a uniform consistency then process about 10–15 seconds to liquefy somewhat. Taste and adjust seasonings. Refrigerate for 4 hours or overnight.

Pepperoni and Pasta Soup

Makes 6–8 servings

3 tablespoons olive oil
1 medium onion, minced
1 clove garlic, minced
1 (14.5-ounce) can
    medium pitted black
    olives, drained and
    chopped
1 (8-ounce) jar stuffed
    green olives, drained
    and chopped
1 tablespoon capers,
    drained and chopped
8 ounces mushrooms,
    canned or fresh,
    chopped
3.5 ounces pepperoni,
    chopped
2 (8-ounce) cans tomato
    sauce
4 cups water
1 tablespoon plus 1 tea-
    spoon beef base
2 teaspoons basil
1 teaspoon oregano
1 tablespoon sugar
$1^{1}/_{2}$–2 cups broken spa-
    ghetti or spaghettini
Parmesan cheese

In a large soup pot, heat oil until shimmery then add the onion and garlic and saute 3–4 minutes, stirring frequently. Add the olives and capers and saute 3 minutes more.

Add all remaining ingredients except pasta and cheese and bring to a boil; reduce heat and simmer 5 minutes before adding spaghetti. Maintain a low boil, stirring frequently, until pasta is cooked, about 10 minutes. Add cheese for garnish

Tomato-Basil Soup {V}

Makes 4 *servings*

1 onion, sliced
1–2 tablespoons olive oil
2 (15-ounce) cans
    stewed or crushed
    tomatoes
1/2 teaspoon dried basil
    or 2 tablespoons
    chopped fresh basil
1 (8-ounce) can tomato
    juice or V-8, divided
Salt and pepper

In a medium frying pan, saute onion in oil then transfer to a blender. Pour in tomatoes and basil. Add half the can of juice and blend, stopping to add more juice if the mixture is too thick for the blender to process correctly. Transfer to a medium saucepan and heat. Season with salt and pepper.

Crabby Tomato Cocktail Soup

Makes 8–10 *servings*

4 cups tomato juice
1 (10-ounce) can
    grapefruit, with
    liquid
1 cup claw crabmeat*

Blend tomato juice and grapefruit together briefly to break the grapefruit into tiny pieces. Stir in the crabmeat and serve.

*Canned crabmeat, not imitation.

Broth-Base Soups

Soba Noodles with Spinach and Chicken Soup

Makes 4 servings

2 tablespoons olive oil
1 large onion sliced in
    rings and separated
2 cups chicken broth
$1/4$ cup soy sauce
1 teaspoon grated fresh
    gingerroot
Salt and pepper
2 cups cut-up roasted
    chicken
1 (8-ounce) package
    fresh baby spinach
$1/2$ pound soba noodles,*
    cooked

In a large saucepan, heat oil and saute onions on medium-high heat for 2 minutes, stirring frequently.

Pour in chicken broth. Add soy sauce. Grate gingerroot into pan, about 20–25 strokes over a fine grater; stir broth well to mix. Bring broth to boiling. Adjust salt and pepper, to taste.

Add chicken. Distribute spinach over the broth, cover pan with a lid, and bring liquid to a low rolling boil. Let spinach steam for about 2 minutes, until it wilts.

To serve, divide hot noodles into four bowls. Portion out the soup solids over the noodles and then pour hot broth over the top.

*You can substitute whole wheat spaghetti noodles.

Chicken Wonton Soup

Makes 4 servings

**6 large square egg roll
    wrappers**
4 cups water
**1 tablespoon chicken
    bouillon powder**
**3/4 cup finely minced
    rotisserie chicken**
**1 tablespoon finely
    minced onion**
**1 1/2 teaspoons finely
    minced fresh
    gingerroot**
**1 tablespoon plus
    1 teaspoon
    Worcestershire sauce**
2 teaspoons sugar
1 tablespoon cornstarch
**1 egg wash (1 small
    egg whisked with 1
    tablespoon cold water)**
1 cup grated carrot
**1 (4-ounce) can mush-
    room pieces, drained**
Chives, optional

Place egg roll wrappers on a cutting board in a stack. With a sharp knife, cut stack into 24 smaller squares. Separate for easy use.

Pour water and bouillon into a wide-bottom saucepan and bring to a boil.

Mix together the chicken, onion, gingerroot, Worcestershire sauce, sugar, and cornstarch for the filling.

Fill and twist the wontons one by one, as follows: brush egg wash on the outer half-inch of the wrapper. Spoon a rounded half-teaspoon of filling into the center. Fold up opposite corners and pinch together, then twist closed. Set aside and repeat. Place 6–12 wontons right side up in boiling broth and cook, simmering, for 2 minutes. Spoon broth over the tops as they cook. Transfer 6 cooked wontons to 2 serving bowls with a slotted spoon. Repeat process for other 12 wontons.

Add carrots and mushrooms to the broth and boil for 3 minutes. Divide soup among the four bowls. Sprinkle lightly with chives.

Chinese Egg Drop Soup

Makes 4 servings

2 (14.5-ounce) cans chicken broth
2 teaspoons cornstarch dissolved in 1 table-spoon cold water
2 eggs, lightly beaten
Salt
Pinch freshly grated gingerroot
1 scallion, thinly sliced, both white and green parts

Bring broth to a boil in a medium saucepan. Pour cornstarch mixture into the boiling broth and whisk vigorously while broth thickens and turns clear, about 30 seconds. Slowly pour eggs into the boiling broth then swirl it just once around the pan. Remove from heat and taste for saltiness; adjust. Grate a very small amount of ginger into the soup and stir in. Ladle soup into bowls and garnish with scallion.

Chick Pea with Chard Soup

Makes 4 servings

2 (14.5-ounce) cans chicken broth
1/8 teaspoon garlic salt
1/2 teaspoon dill weed
1/3 cup chopped pancetta*
1 (15-ounce) can chick peas, drained and rinsed
1 bunch chard, roughly chopped
Salt and pepper

In a large deep skillet, heat broth, garlic salt, dill weed, pancetta, and chick peas to boiling. Reduce heat and cover; simmer 5 minutes. Add chard to the pan and stir into the liquid. Cover again and let steam for 3–4 minutes. Add salt and pepper, to taste, and adjust seasonings.

*You can substitute finely diced deli ham.

Easy French Onion Soup

Makes 4 servings

3–4 medium yellow
    onions, halved and
    sliced
2 tablespoons olive oil
1 tablespoon butter
2 cups chicken broth
1 cup water
2 teaspoons beef base
1/4 teaspoon ground
    marjoram
Seasoned croutons
1/2 cup grated Parmesan
    cheese

In a medium saucepan, saute onions in oil and butter for 15–20 minutes, stirring frequently, until they caramelize. Add all remaining ingredients, except the croutons and cheese; cover pan and simmer soup for 20 minutes while flavors meld.

To serve, drop 3–4 seasoned croutons into the bottom of each bowl. Ladle soup over the croutons and top with cheese.

Curried Cream of Chicken Soup

Makes 4 servings

4 tablespoons butter
4 tablespoons flour
1 teaspoon curry
    powder
2 (14.5-ounce) cans
    chicken broth
1 cup half-and-half
Salt

Melt butter in a medium saucepan then stir in flour and curry to make roux. Cook for 2 minutes, stirring. Whisk broth into the roux a little at a time. Bring to a boil, stirring frequently. Add half-and-half and heat without boiling. Season with salt, if desired.

Easy Cheesy Soup {V}

Makes 4 servings

1 (14.5-ounce) can vegetable broth
1¼ cups milk
1 tablespoon cornstarch
2 tablespoons half-and-half
1¼ cups grated cheddar jack cheese or ¾ cup grated sharp cheddar
Pepper
¼ teaspoon paprika
½ cup potato flakes, optional

Heat broth and milk in a medium saucepan over medium-high heat until just about boiling. In a small bowl, stir cornstarch into half-and-half to dissolve. Add cornstarch mixture to the soup and whisk constantly as the soup comes to a low boil while it thickens. Stir in cheese until melted. Season with pepper and paprika. If you want a slightly thicker soup, add potato flakes and mix well.

Sesame–Cooking Greens Soup

Makes 4 servings

3 cups water
½ bunch collards
1 teaspoon beef base
½ pound beef steak, sliced very thinly and chopped
½ cup diced white onion
1 clove garlic, minced
¼ teaspoon freshly grated gingerroot

½ teaspoon sesame oil
Salt

Bring water to a boil in a medium saucepan. Chop collard leaves roughly and place in boiling water; cook 5 minutes, or until leaves are tender. Add all remaining ingredients except salt, and stir. Reduce heat, cover, and let simmer for 15–20 minutes, until onion is tender. Add salt, to taste, and adjust seasonings.

Udon Noodle Soup

Makes 4 servings

1 (10-ounce) package
   Japanese udon
   noodles
3 tablespoons Memmi
   Noodle Soup Base*
2 cups water
1/2 cup shaved carrot
2 scallions, chopped
4 white mushrooms,
   thinly sliced
1/2 cup cooked beef,
   chicken, or pork,
   finely chopped

Cook noodles in water per package directions; drain and set aside. In a medium saucepan, bring Memmi to boil in water. Add all vegetables and meat and boil 2–3 minutes. Remove from heat and add noodles; let sit for 2–3 minutes while they heat. Divide into bowls and serve.

*Find in the Asian food section of your market.

Shrimp and Rice Noodle Soup

Makes 4–6 servings

1 (10-ounce) package
   Chinese rice noodles
4 tablespoons Memmi
   Noodle Soup Base*
3 cups water
2 scallions, chopped
4 ounces sugar snap peas
1 pound cooked shrimp
   (31–40 count)

Cook noodles in water per package directions; let rest in hot water while making the soup. In a medium saucepan, bring Memmi to boil in water. Add scallions and peas and boil lightly for 3 minutes while peas soften. Add shrimp to pan and simmer while they heat through. Divide noodles into bowls and ladle hot soup over top.

*Find in the Asian food section of your market.

Wilted Greens Soup

Makes 4 servings

1 (14.5-ounce) can beef
  broth
1 (14.5-ounce) can
  chicken broth
2 cups water
1 tablespoon dehydrated
  onion flakes
$1/2$ teaspoon grated fresh
  gingerroot
1 teaspoon soy sauce
$1^1/2$ cups cooked white
  or brown rice
4 ounces fresh baby
  spinach
2 cups thinly sliced
  Napa cabbage
1 cup fresh bean sprouts
$1/3$ bunch cilantro,
  chopped
$1/2$ cup diced deli meat
  of choice, optional

In a medium saucepan, bring
broths and water to a boil over
medium-high heat with onion,
gingerroot, and soy sauce. Add rice
and reduce to a low boil for 2–3
minutes. Add spinach, cabbage,
sprouts, and cilantro, and submerge in the broth. Let broth bubble for 2–4 minutes, until greens
are wilted. Stir in meat, if using.

Spring Soup

Makes 4 servings

4–6 spring onions,
   trimmed and chopped,
   white and green parts
1 parsnip, finely
   chopped
1 carrot, finely chopped
1 tablespoon olive oil
1 tablespoon butter
2 cups baby kale,
   stems discarded and
   roughly chopped
2 (14.5-ounce) cans
   chicken broth
1 tablespoon plus 1 tea-
   spoon fresh lime juice
$^1/_2$ cup chopped cilantro
$^1/_2$ teaspoon salt
Pinch pepper

In a medium frying pan, saute onion, parsnip, and carrot in hot oil and butter on medium heat for 5 minutes, or until vegetables are slightly tender. Add kale and stir to coat; saute 3 more minutes. Meanwhile, heat broth to boiling in a medium saucepan over medium-high heat. Add vegetables and juice to the soup and bring to a boil again. Remove from heat and stir in cilantro. Season with salt and pepper.

VARIATION: This recipe can be made with any of the earliest vegetables from the garden, such as radishes, spinach, asparagus, or over-wintered greens or root vegetables.

Mongolian Hot Pot

Makes 6–8 servings

4–8 ounces cellophane
   noodles or Chinese
   rice noodles

Dipping Sauce

3 tablespoons soy sauce
2 teaspoons sesame oil
2 teaspoons brown sugar
2 teaspoons water
$1/2$ teaspoon rice vinegar

Soup Solids

2 pounds very thinly
   sliced* meat and/or
   seafood, cut in bite-
   size lengths (sirloin
   steak, lean pork,
   ham, chicken breast,
   shell-on shrimp
   (31-40 count), firm-
   fleshed fish
2–2$1/2$ pounds vegetables,
   trimmed and sliced
   or cut in bite-size
   pieces (Napa or savoy
   cabbage, spinach or
   chard leaves, mush-
   rooms, bean sprouts)
1 (16-ounce) package
   firm tofu, drained, cut
   into $1/2$-inch squares

Broth

6 cups chicken stock
$1/4$ cup soy sauce
2 scallions, chopped
1 clove garlic, finely
   minced
1 tablespoon peeled and
   finely grated fresh
   gingerroot
1 tablespoon sesame oil

Prepare the noodles according to package directions, but do not cook all the way; leave al dente. Drain and then cover with cold water.

Bring all the dipping sauce ingredients to a simmer in a small saucepan over medium heat. Stir and remove from heat. Divide into 6–8 small portions

Arrange the prepared meats and vegetables in overlapping rows on a tray for easy use.

Wafer-thin meat and thinly sliced vegetables and tofu cook very quickly (anywhere from 30 to 90 seconds, to taste) in constantly simmering broth. If you have a hot pot, use it at the table and let everyone cook their own meat and vegetables, dipping into the broth a little at a time so it keeps boiling. Retrieve with chopsticks or a wire strainer. Otherwise, you can achieve a similar flavor by cooking meat and vegetables in small batches on the stove. Add partially cooked noodles to the broth after the meat and vegetables are all cooked. Divide solid ingredients among bowls and pour hot broth over each serving. Serve dipping sauce on the side.

*Freeze chicken, beef, and pork for 30 minutes to make slicing easier or have your butcher do the slicing for you.

Spicy Tomato Consomme

Makes 8 servings

4 cups tomato juice
1 (14.5-ounce) can beef consomme
1 teaspoon lemon juice
1 teaspoon Worcestershire sauce
$1/4$ teaspoon horseradish
1–2 dashes hot sauce, optional

In a medium saucepan, heat all ingredients except hot sauce together and bring just to a simmer. Remove from heat, taste, and add hot sauce, if desired.

Potato
Soups

Vichyssoise {V}

2 tablespoons olive oil
4 tablespoons butter
4 leeks, finely sliced
4 medium-size russet
    potatoes, peeled and
    chopped
2 teaspoons salt
Water
1 cup whipping cream
Sour cream
Freshly snipped chives

In a large saucepan, heat oil and butter over medium-low heat. Saute leeks for 5–7 minutes, stirring frequently to avoid browning. Add potatoes, salt, and water to cover. Place lid on pan and bring to a boil. Reduce heat to a medium boil for 20–25 minutes, until potatoes are cooked; remove from heat. Puree soup in small batches. Return to pan and stir in cream. Refrigerate or let come to room temperature before serving. Garnish each serving with sour cream and chives.

Poor Man's Soup {V}

Makes 6 servings

2 tablespoons olive oil
1 medium onion, chopped
3 large potatoes, cubed
Water
2 tablespoons butter
1 cup milk
1–2 teaspoons salt
1/2 teaspoon pepper

In a medium saucepan, heat the oil over medium-high heat. Add onion and saute about 4 minutes, until it turns translucent. Add potatoes and enough hot tap water to almost cover. Fit a lid on the pan and bring to a low boil. Cook 25–30 minutes, until potatoes are cooked and the water begins to thicken. Stir frequently to prevent scorching. When potatoes are done, add butter and milk, and heat through. Taste and add salt and pepper.

Corn Chowder

Makes 10–12 *servings*

1/2 **pound smoked bacon**
1 **large onion, finely diced**
3 **ribs celery, finely diced**
3 **pounds russet potatoes, peeled, and diced**
3 **(14.5-ounce) cans corn, with liquid**
2 **(14.5-ounce) cans chicken broth**
1 **tablespoon salt**
Water
1 **pint whipping cream**
White pepper

Dice bacon before cooking. Over medium-high heat, crisp bacon in a medium frying pan without letting it burn. Remove bacon to paper towels to drain, reserving the bacon fat. Set bacon aside or refrigerate. Continue heating the fat on low until the solids sink to the bottom. Carefully pour the clarified fat into a large soup pot without the solid bits.

Saute onion and celery in the fat over medium heat, stirring frequently, until onion turns translucent. Add potatoes, corn, broth, salt, and enough water to almost cover. Place lid on pot and bring soup to a boil; reduce to a moderate boil and cook for 30 minutes, stirring frequently until potatoes are fork-tender. Stir in cream and adjust seasoning with salt and pepper. Garnish individual servings with crumbled bacon.

Potato with Ham and Mustard Soup

Makes 8–10 *servings*

3 pounds red potatoes, peeled and diced

1 cup diced celery

Water

2 (14.5-ounce) cans corn, drained

2 cups diced ham

1½ teaspoons dry mustard

2 tablespoons prepared honey mustard

1 teaspoon Worcestershire sauce

1 teaspoon chicken bouillon powder

¼ teaspoon pepper

2 cups milk

In a large saucepan, cover potatoes and celery with water. Bring to a boil over high heat, then reduce to medium and cook potatoes until soft. Add all remaining ingredients except milk. Let cook about 5 minutes more, stirring occasionally. Add milk and heat through.

NOTE: The water will thicken as the potatoes continue to cook, so usually no other thickener is needed.

Bacon-Blue Potato Soup

Makes 6 servings

4 strips bacon, diced
2 tablespoons butter
2 teaspoons chicken
  bouillon powder
1/4 cup crumbled blue
  cheese
4 cups leftover mashed
  potatoes*
1/4 cup ranch dressing
1 1/2 cups milk
1/2 cup whipping cream
Pepper

Cook bacon in a medium saucepan and discard all but 2 tablespoons of the fat. Add butter, bouillon, and cheese; melt together. Add the potatoes, dressing, and milk; mix together. Cover the pan and heat on medium, stirring frequently, until the potatoes are heated through. Stir in the cream. If you want a thinner soup, add more milk. Season with pepper, to taste.

*Try using blue potatoes to make this soup extra fun to eat

Ham and Cheese Baked Potato Soup

Makes 8–10 servings

6 medium-size russet
  potatoes, baked
6 tablespoons butter
2 green onions, sliced
2 cups minced ham
2 cups grated cheddar
  cheese, divided
1 cup sour cream
Salt and pepper
3–4 cups milk

Scoop cooked potato from the skins into a large saucepan and discard skins. Mash with a potato masher, if desired. Fold in all remaining ingredients except 1/2 cup cheese and milk. Now stir in 3 cups milk and heat on medium-high, stirring frequently, until soup is hot. If too thick, add rest of milk. Adjust seasonings. Garnish individual servings with remaining cheese.

Loaded Baked Potato Soup

Makes 4 servings

2 baked russet potatoes, diced with peel

4 tablespoons sour cream

1 tablespoon bacon grease

1 cup half-and-half

¾ cup grated cheddar jack cheese

1 tablespoon butter

2 tablespoons crispy cooked bacon

Salt and pepper

1 tablespoon chopped chives

Place potatoes, sour cream, bacon grease, and half-and-half in a medium microwave-safe bowl. Cover bowl and microwave on 80 percent power for 3 minutes. Remove bowl and add remaining ingredients except chives; mix together. Cover bowl and microwave on full power for 3 more minutes. Remove carefully and mix ingredients again. Serve garnished with chives.

Chunky Potato Soup {V}

Makes 6–8 *servings*

**2 large carrots, peeled
and sliced
1 rib celery, sliced
1/4 cup finely chopped
onion
1 1/2 cups water
1/2 cup butter
1/2 cup flour
2 teaspoons salt
1/2 teaspoon pepper
8 cups milk
2 large baking potatoes,
baked and cut into
1-inch cubes with
peel
Grated cheddar cheese**

In a small saucepan, bring carrots, celery, onion, and water to a boil then reduce heat to low. Let vegetables simmer while you prepare the soup.

In a large heavy-bottom saucepan or Dutch oven, melt butter over medium-high heat. Whisk in flour, salt, and pepper; stir and cook for 1 minute. The mixture will look like a thick paste. Slowly whisk in milk, and stir continuously until thickened, approximately 20 minutes. Reduce heat and add potatoes. Transfer vegetables to soup, reserving the cooking liquid. Stir and simmer for 5 minutes. If soup gets too thick, thin with some of the reserved liquid. Serve with a sprinkle of cheese.

German Potato Soup

Makes 8–10 servings

6 medium potatoes,
  peeled and cubed
1 medium onion, diced
4–5 cups water
$1/2$ pound bacon, sliced
  crosswise into thin
  strips
4 rounded tablespoons
  flour
$3/4$ cup sour cream
1 (14.5-ounce) can
  chicken broth
2 cups milk, divided
2 tablespoons white
  vinegar
1 tablespoon chicken
  bouillon powder
1 teaspoon celery seed
Salt and pepper
4 hard-boiled eggs,
  chopped
Chopped pimiento

In a large saucepan, boil potatoes
and onion in water until tender;
drain.

Meanwhile, cook bacon over
medium heat in another large
covered saucepan. Drain off all but
4 tablespoons of the fat. Stir flour
into the bacon and fat and cook on
low heat for 2–3 minutes. Stir in the
sour cream and then the chicken
broth to make a roux.

Add potatoes and onions to the
bacon and fold together. Add 1 cup
milk and mix well. Add all remaining ingredients, except egg and
pimiento, and the rest of the milk,
if desired. Heat and serve with a
sprinkling of eggs and pimiento.

Zuppa Toscana

Makes 8–10 servings

1 large onion, diced
1 1/2 pounds mild Italian
    ground sausage*
6–7 large red potatoes,
    peeled, quartered
    and thinly sliced
2 (14.5-ounce) cans
    chicken broth
4 cups water
1–2 teaspoons red chile
    flakes
1 pint whipping cream
1 large bunch kale,
    tough stems removed
    and leaves chopped
Chicken bouillon
    powder

In a large soup pot, brown the onion and sausage; drain fat. Add potatoes, broth, water, and chile flakes. Cover pot and bring to a boil for about 20 minutes, until potatoes are tender. Stir in the cream. Soup will thicken the longer you keep it warm and stirred. Mix kale into hot soup for about the last 5 minutes of cooking. Taste and adjust seasoning with small addition of bouillon, if desired.

*Italian ground turkey can be substituted.

NOTE: This recipe is inspired by the Olive Garden soup of the same name.

Potato and Parsnip Soup

Makes 4 servings

1/2 cup chopped onion
2 teaspoons bacon
  grease
1 tablespoon olive oil
1 large potato, peeled
  and chopped
2 cups water
1 Knorr chicken bouillon
  cube or 2 teaspoons
  bouillon powder
2 cups peeled and
  chopped parsnips
1/2 cup whipping cream
2 cups milk
1 tablespoon butter
1/2 teaspoon nutmeg
1/8 teaspoon pepper
Salt
1 tablespoon cornstarch
  dissolved in 2
  tablespoons water

In a medium nonstick saucepan, saute onion in bacon grease and olive oil for 3 minutes. Add potato and saute 3 minutes more. Add water, bouillon, and parsnips. Cover and bring to a low boil; simmer for 20 minutes, until potatoes are cooked. Add all remaining ingredients except cornstarch mixture. Bring to a boil then thicken with mixture, stirring constantly.

Creamy Pesto Potato Soup

Makes 6–8 *servings*

Pesto

2 tightly packed cups
    fresh basil leaves
2–3 cloves garlic, sliced
1/2 cup light walnut
    halves
1/2 cup grated Parmesan
    or Asiago cheese
1/2–3/4 cup extra virgin
    olive oil

Soup

1 small onion, finely
    chopped
2 tablespoons olive oil
2 tablespoons butter
6 medium-size russet
    potatoes, peeled and
    sliced
2 Knorr chicken
    bouillon cubes
Water
1 1/2–2 cups half-and-half
    or whipping cream
Salt and pepper

Make the pesto in a food processor or blender. Pulse basil, garlic, walnuts, and cheese together 2–3 times, then process continuously while adding oil to form a spreadable mixture.

In a large saucepan, saute onion in oil and butter until it turns translucent. Add potatoes and bouillon and cover with water. Cover pan and bring potatoes to a boil; reduce heat and cook at a low boil for 20–25 minutes, until potatoes are fork-tender. Using a hand-held mixer, blend potatoes in cooking liquid until creamy. Add half the pesto and 1 cup half-and-half. Blend with mixer. Taste and continue adding pesto, half-and-half, and salt and pepper, to taste. Refrigerate or freeze any remaining pesto for another dish.

Sour Cream Potato Soup

Makes 8–10 servings

2 medium onions,
   chopped
1/2 cup butter
6 russet potatoes,
   peeled and sliced
3–4 cups water
1 (12-ounce) can
   evaporated milk
2 (14.5-ounce) cans
   chicken broth
4 eggs, beaten
1 (8-ounce) package less-
   fat cream cheese,
   room temperature
2 tablespoons flour
1 (16-ounce) container
   fat-free sour cream
Salt and pepper

In a medium frying pan, saute onions in butter over medium heat until onions are brown on the edges. Remove from heat.

In a large saucepan, boil potatoes in enough water to almost cover for about 25 minutes, until tender. Pour off most of the water and mash the potatoes. Add onions, milk, and chicken broth to the potatoes and fold in; bring to a boil. Combine eggs and cream cheese; temper by stirring 1/2 cup hot potato mixture into the cream cheese, and then combine cream cheese mixture with the potatoes. Whisk flour into the sour cream and stir into the soup. Reheat if needed. Season with salt and pepper, to taste.

Garlicky Potato Dumpling Stew

Makes 6 servings

- 1 (16-ounce) package gnocchi
- 1 (14.5-ounce) can vegetable broth
- 2 cups water
- 1 tablespoon vegetable bouillon powder
- 1 tablespoon plus 1 teaspoon chicken bouillon powder
- 3–4 tablespoons basil pesto
- 2 cups half-and-half
- 2 tablespoons cornstarch dissolved in 4 tablespoons water
- 1/2 teaspoon salt
- 1/8 teaspoon pepper
- Parmesan cheese

In a medium saucepan, cook gnocchi according to package directions. When dumplings float to the top, they're done. Drain water and transfer gnocchi to a bowl while you make the soup.

In the same saucepan, place all the remaining ingredients except cheese. Bring to a boil over high heat, stirring constantly then reduce to low. Return gnocchi back to the pan and let soup simmer for 1–2 minutes while dumplings reheat. Serve with a sprinkling of cheese for garnish.

Poultry
Soups

Homemade Chicken Broth

Makes about 3 quarts broth

4 large skinless and boneless chicken breast halves
3 quarts water
1/2 onion
2 teaspoons salt

Place all ingredients in a large soup pot and bring to a boil. Cook for about 1 hour, until chicken is cooked through and becomes tender enough to split apart with a fork. Remove from heat; discard onion. Transfer chicken pieces to a plate or work surface to cool. Cut or tear the chicken into pieces for recipes. Refrigerate the pan broth overnight; remove solid fat the next day and use the remaining broth for soups, gravies, or sauces. Broth can be refrigerated for 4–5 days or frozen for up to a year.

Country-Style Chicken Noodle Soup

Makes 4–6 *servings*

2 (14.5-ounce) cans
  chicken broth
3 cups water
2 teaspoons Knorr
  bouillon powder
1 small onion, chopped
3 carrots, sliced
4 stalks celery, sliced
1 bay leaf
1 (14.5-ounce) can corn,
  drained
2 1/2 cups cut-up roasted
  chicken
2 teaspoons salt
1/4 teaspoon pepper
8 ounces wide egg
  noodles

Bring broth and water to a boil in a large saucepan. Add bouillon, onion, carrots, celery, and bay leaf. Cover pan and boil on medium heat until vegetables are tender, about 15 minutes. Add corn, chicken, salt, and pepper; return to boiling for 2 minutes. Add noodles to the soup; cook at a medium boil until noodles are al dente, about 7 minutes. Remove pan from heat and keep covered until ready to serve. Noodles will continue to soften in the hot broth.

Chicken Noodleless Soup

Makes 6–8 *servings*

1 cup shredded cabbage

1/2 pound pork sausage, browned and drained

1 1/2 cups shredded rotisserie chicken

2 tablespoons Knorr chicken bouillon powder

1/2 teaspoon ground sage

1/8 teaspoon garlic powder

1 small onion, roughly chopped

3 medium russet potatoes, scrubbed and diced

1 red bell pepper, diced

2 golden delicious apples, cored and diced

6 cups water

Salt and pepper

Place all ingredients in a large soup pot and bring to a boil. Reduce to simmer for 30–45 minutes while vegetables cook and flavors meld. Taste and adjust seasoning with salt, pepper, and bouillon by the half teaspoon, if more flavor is needed.

Chicken Gumbo

Makes 4 servings

1 quart chicken broth
1/2 pound ground pork
    sausage, browned
    and drained
1 medium onion, chopped
4 stalks celery, sliced
1 green bell pepper,
    diced
5 medium tomatoes,
    peeled, seeded, and
    chopped or 1 (14-
    ounce) can diced
    tomatoes, drained
8 fresh okra pods, ends
    removed and thinly
    sliced or 3/4 cup
    frozen okra
1/2 cup uncooked brown
    rice
2 small bay leaves
1 teaspoon Cajun
    seasoning
2 teaspoons salt
1 1/2 cups shredded
    rotisserie chicken
2 tablespoons flour
    mixed with 2 table-
    spoons melted butter
Hot sauce

Place all ingredients except chicken, flour-butter mixture, and hot sauce in a large saucepan. Stir together and bring to a boil over medium-high heat. Reduce heat to medium and continue simmering for about 35 minutes, until rice is cooked. Add chicken and flour mixture, and whisk to break up the flour. Continue simmering about 10 minutes more. Taste and adjust seasoning; add a few drops of hot sauce, if desired.

Simple Chicken and Dumplings

Makes 4 servings

2 (14.5-ounce) cans fat-free chicken broth
2 cups grated carrot
2 (14.5-ounce) cans cream of chicken soup, condensed
2 cups shredded or cubed precooked chicken
1 (16.3 ounce) can large (grande) refrigerator biscuits
Pepper
Parsley

Pour broth into a wide-bottom large soup pot and heat to boiling. Add carrot and bring back to a boil. Whisk in soup, then add chicken and bring to a boil. Set all 8 biscuits in the broth (squeeze them together if your pan isn't wide enough for a comfortable fit), cover with a lid, and reduce heat to medium-low. Steam the biscuits in simmering soup for 8–10 minutes without removing the lid.

To serve, lift biscuits from pot into serving bowls then ladle soup over the biscuits. Sprinkle with pepper and parsley.

Chicken and Corn Chowder

Makes 4–6 *servings*

2 medium russet
  potatoes, peeled
  and diced
3 slices yellow onion,
  diced
2 stalks celery, diced
2 teaspoons dried
  parsley
Water
2 rounded teaspoons
  chicken bouillon
  powder
1/4 teaspoon pepper
2 (15-ounce) cans corn,
  drained
3 slices bacon, browned
  and crumbled,
  optional
1 1/2 cups diced roasted
  chicken
4 tablespoons butter or
  bacon grease
4 tablespoons flour
1/2 cup half-and-half

Place potatoes, onion, celery, and parsley with enough water to cover in a medium soup pot. Cook until tender, about 25–30 minutes. Add bouillon, pepper, corn, bacon, and chicken and heat.

While heating soup, melt butter or grease in a small frying pan and add the flour to make roux. Cook, stirring frequently to prevent burning, until flour starts to brown, about 4 minutes. Ladle about 1/4 cup liquid from the soup into the flour and gently stir until liquid is absorbed; repeat with another 1/4 cup liquid.

Pour half-and-half into soup. Add roux and gently whisk till roux is blended into the soup. Let cook, stirring, about 3 minutes while the soup thickens.

Chicken Mushroom Soup

Makes 6–8 *servings*

3 stalks celery, thinly sliced
8 ounces sliced mushrooms
1 tablespoon olive oil
1 teaspoon butter
1 (11-ounce) package Uncle Ben's White & Wild Rice (quick cooking)
1 tablespoon Knorr chicken bouillon powder
¼ teaspoon pepper
1½ cups shredded cooked chicken
4 cups water

In a medium frying pan, saute celery and mushrooms in oil and butter for 5 to 7 minutes, until celery begins to soften.

Cook rice in a medium saucepan according to package directions, except leave out the oil and butter. Then add all remaining ingredients plus vegetables into the rice pan; let simmer 5 minutes while flavors meld. Serve hot.

Easy Chicken Curry Stew

Makes 6–8 *servings*

1 stick butter
5 tablespoons flour
2 cups frozen hash
    browns
1 (16-ounce) package
    frozen mixed
    vegetables (peas,
    carrots, corn, beans)
1 (14.5-ounce) can
    chicken broth
4 cups water
2 rounded teaspoons
    chicken bouillon
    powder
2 tablespoons dehydrated
    onion flakes
1 teaspoon nutmeg
1 teaspoon curry powder
2 cups shredded
    rotisserie chicken
1/2 pint whipping cream
    or 1 cup milk

To make roux, melt butter in a small frying pan and stir in flour. Cook over medium heat, stirring frequently, for 3–4 minutes while the flour cooks.

Place all remaining ingredients except chicken and cream in a medium saucepan and bring to a boil; reduce heat to medium and let simmer for 3–4 minutes to thaw the vegetables. Whisk in the roux and combine well; broth will thicken. Bring to a boil and add chicken and cream then reduce heat to low and simmer for 2–3 minutes. Taste for chicken flavor. If needed, add 1 teaspoon of bouillon powder.

Chicken Pot Pie Stew

2 pounds skinless and boneless chicken breasts or thighs, cut into bite-size chunks
1 teaspoon salt
2 (14.5-ounce) cans cream of chicken soup, condensed
1 (14.5-ounce) can cream of mushroom soup, condensed
1 (16-ounce) package frozen mixed vegetables
1½ cups southern-style hash browns, thawed
1½ cups Bisquick
¾ cup milk

In a large bowl, mix together the chicken chunks, salt, and soups, then place into a medium-size or larger slow cooker. Cook on low for 6–8 hours. About 1 hour before serving, stir vegetables and hash browns into the chicken mixture. Stir Bisquick and milk together in a medium bowl then spoon tablespoon-size dumplings over the chicken mixture. Cover and turn slow cooker to high for 1–1½ hours.

Two-day Chicken Rack Soup

Makes 4 servings

2 chicken racks* and
  skin
6 cups water
1 small onion
3 carrots, peeled and
  sliced
2 potatoes, peeled and
  cubed
3 stalks celery, sliced
1 bay leaf
2 teaspoons salt
$1/2$ teaspoon pepper
1 (14.5-ounce) can
  chicken broth,
  optional
1–2 cups shredded or
  diced precooked
  chicken
1 teaspoon chicken
  bouillon powder

Place chicken racks in a 5-quart or larger slow cooker and nearly cover with water. Cook on high for about 2 hours, until boiling; turn to low and let simmer for 2 hours more (about 4 hours total). Turn off cooker; remove and discard solids with a slotted spoon. Refrigerate the stock overnight. The next day, lift the solid grease from the broth and discard it. The stock will likely be a solid gel. Let crock warm to room temperature.

Turn slow cooker to high until gel is liquefied. Meantime, add all vegetables and seasonings. If more liquid is needed to cover, add 1 can chicken broth. Let cook 3–4 hours on low. Add chicken during last 1–2 hours of cooking. Taste soup for seasonings. If broth seems weak, add bouillon 1 teaspoon at a time until it suits your palate. Stir well and taste after each addition.

*Bones and skin make a delicious soup stock. Save bones and skin from rotisserie chickens in the freezer until you have two or more for this soup.

Kay's Three-Day Chicken Soup

Makes 10–12 servings

**1 whole chicken, frozen
(if thawed, skip to
the boiling)**
Water
**2 medium onions,
chopped**
1 bunch celery, sliced
**Chicken bouillon cubes,
to taste**
**8–16 ounces noodles
(depending whether
you want more
noodles or more
broth)**
**Chopped fresh green
onion**

DAY 1: Take whole chicken out of freezer and defrost in refrigerator.

DAY 2: Throw away innards. Cut chicken into large pieces. In a large soup pot, boil chicken in water to cover for 1 hour or until you can easily pierce the meat with little resistance. Transfer chicken pieces to a baking sheet to cool. Cool and skim the broth. Discard skin and bones; break chicken into pieces. Refrigerate broth and chicken overnight, in separate containers.

DAY 3: Remove solid fat from broth. Add water to double the amount of broth. Add onions, celery, and bouillon, to taste. Boil about 1 hour. Add chicken and noodles and boil 15 minutes, until noodles are just tender. Taste and adjust seasoning.

Serve with a light garnish of green onion.

Apricot Chicken Curry Soup

Makes 6 servings

1/2 medium onion, diced

2 stalks celery, sliced

2 apples, diced

3/4 cup dried apricots, chopped

3 tablespoons butter

1 rounded tablespoon curry powder

1 teaspoon mustard seed

1/4 teaspoon ground bay leaf

1 teaspoon ground ginger

1 teaspoon Season-All

1/2 teaspoon ground allspice

1/4 teaspoon ground cloves

1/8 teaspoon garlic powder

2 teaspoons chicken bouillon powder

1/4 cup flour

2 (14.5-ounce) cans chicken broth

1 tablespoon cider vinegar

3 cups cut-up rotisserie chicken

3/4 cup coconut milk

1 cup cooked rice

In a medium saucepan, saute onion, celery, apples, and apricots in butter for about 5 minutes, stirring occasionally. Add all spices and seasonings, plus flour, and stir into the vegetables. Add broth, vinegar, and chicken. Bring to a low boil, cover, and let simmer for 15 minutes, stirring every few minutes. Stir in coconut milk and rice.

Chicken Fajita Soup

Makes 6–8 *servings*

2 large boneless, skinless chicken breasts, trimmed of fat

2 tablespoons vegetable oil

1 medium onion, cut in thin wedges and separated

2 large red bell peppers, sliced lengthwise and cut into shorter pieces

1½ teaspoons fajita spice mix

2 (14-ounce) cans chicken broth

2 teaspoons cornstarch mixed into 1 tablespoon water

¾ cup prepared guacamole

1 cup sour cream

Grated cheddar jack cheese

4–6 flour tortillas

Slice chicken lengthwise, thinly, and cut into pieces about 1½ inches long. Set aside.

In a medium saucepan, heat oil on medium high, then stir-fry onion and bell pepper for 3 minutes, turning vegetables frequently. Add chicken and spice mix. Continue sauteing on medium to high heat, stirring frequently, for 5–7 minutes, until chicken pieces are nearly cooked.

Add broth to pan, cover with a lid, and heat to boiling. Reduce heat and let simmer 15 minutes. Add cornstarch and bring liquid to a boil; stir while it thickens. Mix guacamole and sour cream into the soup and stir to dissolve. Reheat to boiling, then remove pan from heat.

Ladle soup into bowls. Garnish with cheese and serve with warm tortillas.

Lemon Chicken Soup

Makes 8–10 *servings*

Greek Rice Pilaf

3 tablespoons olive oil
3 tablespoons butter
1 cup finely chopped
    onion
2 cups uncooked long
    grain white rice
4 cups chicken broth
½ cup lemon juice
1½ teaspoons dried
    oregano
2 teaspoons salt

The Soup

3 boneless and skinless
    chicken breasts,
    trimmed
6 cups water
Chicken bouillon powder
Salt and pepper
Grated lemon zest

FOR THE PILAF: In a medium saucepan, heat the oil and butter over medium heat and saute the onion for 5–7 minutes, stirring, until onion turns translucent. Add rest of pilaf ingredients and cover pan. Bring to a boil then reduce heat and simmer for 30 minutes, or until rice is soft to the bite. Stir occasionally so rice doesn't stick. Reserve 2–3 cups rice for the soup.

FOR THE SOUP: Slice the chicken breasts lengthwise about ½ inch thick then dice. Place soup ingredients in a large saucepan and bring quickly to a boil. Reduce to a low boil and let cook for 30–40 minutes, until chicken is tender. Skim fat solids from the broth. Add rice to the soup and add more water, if desired. Taste and adjust seasonings with bouillon, salt, and pepper. Garnish each bowl of soup with zest, if desired.

Chicken and Gnocchi Soup

Makes 10 servings

2 tablespoons olive oil
1 tablespoon butter
3 ribs celery, diced small
2 cloves garlic, minced
2 large carrots, grated
$^1/_3$ cup flour
2$^1/_2$ cups diced cooked
  chicken
2 quarts chicken broth
2 cups half-and-half
1 cup whipping cream
1$^1/_2$ tablespoons cornstarch mixed with 2
  tablespoons water
1 pound potato gnocchi
  with Parmesan, or
  plain
6 ounces fresh spinach,
  chopped
2 teaspoons chicken
  bouillon powder,
  optional
Pepper

In a medium saucepan, heat olive oil and butter over medium heat. Saute celery and garlic for about 3 minutes then add carrots and continue sauteing about 2 minutes more. Add flour and toss with vegetables to distribute. Continue cooking about 4 minutes, stirring occasionally, while vegetables soften and flour cooks.

Add chicken and broth; bring to a boil. Add half-and-half and cream and heat on medium until boiling. Thicken broth with cornstarch mixture, stirring rapidly to avoid lumps. Reduce heat to low.

Cook gnocchi according to package directions. As gnocchi float to the top, transfer them with a slotted spoon to the soup. Increase heat to medium high, stirring, until soup begins to bubble. Add spinach and stir in. Let cook for about 1 minute then taste soup. Season with bouillon and pepper, to taste.

NOTE: This soup is inspired by one from the Olive Garden.

Best Cream of Chicken Noodle Soup

Makes 6–8 *servings*

2 large boneless, skin-
   less chicken breasts
1 small onion, chopped
4 ribs celery, sliced
1 (16-ounce) bag mini
   carrots, cut in half
Water
1 (12-ounce) can
   evaporated milk
1 pound wide egg noodles
1–3 teaspoons chicken
   bouillon powder
Pepper

In a large soup pot, cover chicken, onion, celery, and carrots with water and heat on high until boiling; reduce to medium and cook 40–45 minutes, until the chicken is tender. Remove from heat and transfer chicken to a cutting board to cool. When cool enough to handle, cut or tear chicken into bite-size pieces.

Return chicken to the pot and add milk and noodles. Bring to a boil and cook about 10 minutes, stirring occasionally, until noodles are done. Adjust flavor with 1-teaspoon additions of bouillon and pepper until the flavor suits your taste.

Chinese Chicken Noodle Soup

Makes 6 servings

1 (10-ounce) package
  Chinese noodles
6–8 ounces button
  mushrooms, stemmed
  and sliced
1 tablespoon vegetable
  oil
2 (14.5-ounce) cans
  chicken broth
1 1/2 cups cooked
  chicken, very thinly
  sliced and cut into
  1/2-inch squares
1 (5-ounce) can water
  chestnuts, drained
  and julienned
1 green onion, thinly
  sliced, white and
  green parts
3 cups thinly sliced
  Napa cabbage
2 teaspoons soy sauce
6 small sprigs Chinese
  parsley (cilantro)

Cook noodles in water according to package directions then drain in a colander. Dip noodles into cold water to stop the cooking; drain and set aside.

In a medium saucepan, saute mushrooms in oil for about 2 minutes, turning so all sides get cooked. Add broth, chicken, water chestnuts, and onion to the pan and bring to a boil. Add all the cabbage at once and stir to submerge. Boil just until the cabbage wilts, then add noodles to the broth and stir to distribute. Add soy sauce and mix in; taste for saltiness, and adjust if needed.

Use tongs or chopsticks to divide noodles and other solids among individual bowls. Portion broth over top. Garnish each serving with a small sprig of parsley.

Sweet Potato and Chicken Soup

Makes 6 8 *servings*

2 tablespoons olive oil

1 large onion, roughly chopped

1 pound sweet potatoes, cubed

3 medium apples, cored and cubed

1 teaspoon cumin

1 teaspoon dried cilantro leaves

$1/2$ teaspoon turmeric

$1/8$ teaspoon ground cloves

1 (13-ounce) can coconut milk

1 (14.5-ounce) can chicken broth

2 cups cubed cooked chicken

Salt and pepper

Fresh cilantro, chopped

In a medium saucepan, heat the oil on medium-high. Saute the onion about 2 minutes. Add potatoes and apples and continue sauteing, stirring to prevent burning. When the potatoes just begin to soften, stir the spices and herbs into the vegetables and let cook for 1 minute. Add the coconut milk, broth, and chicken; cover the pan and simmer until the vegetables are tender. Season with salt and pepper, to taste. Serve with cilantro for garnish.

Sausage and Chicken Stew

Makes 10–12 servings

- ¾ cup small dried white beans, cleaned
- 4 boneless and skinless chicken thighs cut in bite-size pieces
- 1 tablespoon brown sugar
- ½ teaspoon oregano
- ½ teaspoon chili powder
- ¼ teaspoon garlic powder
- 1 (14.5-ounce) can beef broth
- 1 (14.5-ounce) can stewed or diced tomatoes
- 1 (6-ounce) can tomato paste
- 2 cups water
- 1 Polish kielbasa sausage, cut in slices
- 3–4 tablespoons smoky barbecue sauce
- Salt and pepper

Place the beans in a medium saucepan and cover with water. Bring to a boil and cook for 2–3 minutes. Remove from heat and let beans soak 1–2 hours. Drain.

Place chicken in the bottom of a 3½-quart or larger slow cooker and cover with beans. Sprinkle the sugar, herb, and spices over the beans. Pour in the broth, tomatoes, tomato paste, and water. Cover and turn to low; cook for 6–8 hours, then add sausage and barbecue sauce and cook for another 2 hours. Taste and season with salt and pepper.

Brunswick Stew

Makes 8 servings

4 cups shredded cooked chicken*

6 cups chicken broth

2 russet potatoes, diced

1 (15-ounce) can lima beans, drained

2 (15-ounce) cans corn, drained

2 (14.5-ounce) cans stewed tomatoes

2 tablespoons dehydrated onion flakes

1 teaspoon Cajun spice

1 bay leaf

1 teaspoon seasoned salt

Salt and pepper

Place all ingredients in a large soup pot and bring to a boil. Reduce heat and simmer, covered, for 45 minutes while potatoes cook and flavors meld. Taste and adjust seasonings.

*VARIATION: you can also use shredded pork, beef, or a combination of all.

Autumn Chicken Stew in a Pumpkin

Makes 4–6 *servings*

1 small pumpkin (about 4–5 pounds)

1 cup uncooked brown rice

2 russet potatoes, scrubbed and diced

$1/2$ yellow onion, chopped

1 (14-ounce) can green beans, drained

1 (4-ounce) can sliced mushrooms, drained

1 (14.5-ounce) can cream of chicken soup, condensed

2 cups water

1 (14.5-ounce) can stewed tomatoes

$1^{1}/2$ cups shredded rotisserie chicken

$1/2$ (1.3-ounce) package onion soup and dip mix

2 tablespoons flour

1 teaspoon salt

$1/2$ teaspoon pepper

$1/8$ teaspoon garlic powder

Cut a lid in the pumpkin; remove and discard seeds.

Preheat oven to 375 degrees. Mix all other ingredients in a bowl and then spoon into the pumpkin shell. Place pumpkin on a foil-lined baking sheet and bake, uncovered, for 30 minutes. Remove pumpkin from oven and put the lid in place. Return to oven and bake for 1 hour more. Test for doneness by inserting a fork in the outer skin of the pumpkin; when the fork easily pierces clear through, the dish is ready to eat. Remove from oven and spoon the contents of pumpkin into a serving bowl. Slice wedges of pumpkin and arrange in large soup bowls. Spoon stew over the pumpkin wedges.

Southwest Pumpkin Stew

Makes 12–15 *servings*

2 tablespoons olive oil
1 onion, chopped
3 ribs celery, chopped
3 carrots, diced
2–3 golden delicious
apples, chopped with
skin on
1 (29-ounce) can solid
pumpkin
1 (14.5-ounce) can
chicken broth
1 (15-ounce) can black
beans, drained and
rinsed
2 (15-ounce) cans corn,
drained
2–3 cups diced cooked
chicken
2 teaspoons cumin
2 teaspoons dried
parsley or cilantro
2 teaspoons salt
1/2 teaspoon pepper
1–2 chicken bouillon
cubes, optional

In a large soup pot, heat the oil on medium heat. Saute together the onion, celery, carrots, and apples for about 15 minutes, or until onion is translucent. Raise heat to medium high and stir in the pumpkin and broth; bring to a low boil, stirring occasionally. Add all remaining ingredients and bring soup back to bubbling, stirring occasionally. Reduce heat to low and continue simmering, covered, for about 45 minutes while the flavors meld. Taste and adjust flavor with chicken bouillon, if desired. If too thick, add a small amount of water.

Turkey Burger Soup

Makes 6 servings

3 medium potatoes,
  diced
2 large carrots, sliced
1 rib celery, sliced
8–10 Brussels sprouts,
  trimmed and halved
1 (14.5-ounce) can corn,
  drained
5 cups water
2 teaspoons chicken
  bouillon
1 tablespoon olive oil
3/4 pound ground turkey
1 small onion, chopped
1/2 teaspoon ground sage
1/4 teaspoon whole leaf
  thyme
Salt and pepper
1 (.87-ounce) packet
  turkey gravy mix

Place vegetables, water, and bouillon in a large saucepan. Cover and bring to a boil over medium-high heat; reduce heat to a low boil. Cook until vegetables are tender.

Meanwhile, heat oil in a medium frying pan and brown the turkey, onion, and herbs. Season with salt and pepper. Add turkey to the vegetables and stir in. Test vegetables for doneness; continue cooking until Brussels sprouts are fork-tender, not mushy. Stir in contents of gravy packet and let soup bubble lightly for 2–3 minutes. Taste and adjust seasonings.

Cream of Turkey Noodle Soup

Makes 10–12 *servings*

2 tablespoons olive oil
1 large onion, chopped
1 (2-pound package) whole carrots, peeled and sliced
2 cups sliced celery
12 ounces frozen lima beans
24 ounces frozen corn
2 bay leaves
2 teaspoons rubbed sage
3–4 cups diced cooked turkey
8 cups poultry stock
Water
16 ounces home-style noodles
1 (15-ounce) can low-fat evaporated milk
2 cups turkey gravy*
Chicken bouillon powder
Pepper

In a large soup pot, heat oil over medium-high heat and saute onion until it turns translucent. Add carrots, celery, beans, corn, herbs, and turkey to pot. Pour stock over all and add enough water to cover vegetables by about 2 inches. Cover and bring to a boil; cook until vegetables are tender, about 20 minutes. Add noodles and boil in the soup until noodles are al dente, 10–12 minutes. Add milk and gravy. Heat through then season to taste with chicken bouillon and pepper.

*Can substitute 1 (.87-ounce) packet turkey gravy mix.

Day-After Turkey Soup

Makes 8–10 *servings*

2–3 cups mashed
   potatoes
2 cups stuffing
2–3 cups turkey gravy
2 (14.5-ounce) cans
   chicken broth
2 cups green beans
2 cups cooked sweet
   potatoes, cubed
2 cups other precooked
   vegetables (cauli-
   flower, corn, Brus-
   sels sprouts, greens,
   mushrooms)
2–3 cups diced cooked
   turkey
6 cups water
$1/2$ teaspoon ground sage
Salt and pepper

In a food processor, puree the potatoes, stuffing, and gravy together. Pour into a large sauce-pan, add broth, and bring to a low boil over medium heat, stirring frequently. Add all remaining ingredients except salt and pepper and bring to a low boil again. Reduce heat, cover pan, and simmer for 15–20 minutes. Taste and adjust seasonings with salt and pepper.

Curry Turkey-Rice Soup

1 (14.5-ounce) can
 chicken broth
1/3 cup water
2 cups milk, divided
2 tablespoons butter
2 tablespoons plus
 1 teaspoon flour
1 tablespoon dehydrated
 onion flakes
2 teaspoons (or 2 small
 cubes) chicken
 bouillon
1/2 teaspoon ground sage
1/2 teaspoon whole leaf
 thyme
1 teaspoon curry
 powder
1 heaping cup pre-
 cooked brown rice
1 1/2 cups diced cooked
 turkey
1 1/2 cups frozen peas
 and carrots
Salt and pepper

Heat broth, water, and 1 cup milk to boiling in a large saucepan; reduce heat to simmer. Meanwhile, cook the butter and flour together in a small frying pan for 3–4 minutes to make roux. Thin the roux with small additions of hot broth, stirring each thoroughly into the roux before adding more. After adding about 1 cup of liquid, whisk the roux into the soup until it is well blended; soup will begin to thicken.

Increase heat under the soup to medium-high and add all the remaining ingredients, including the other cup of milk. Stir well and let soup simmer for about 10 minutes while flavors meld and liquid thickens a little more. Season to taste with salt and pepper.

Tomatoey Turkey and Pasta Soup

Makes 6–8 servings

2 medium potatoes, diced
2 large carrots, sliced
2 ribs celery, sliced
6 cups water, divided
1 pound ground turkey
1 medium onion, chopped
1 teaspoon Italian seasoning
1 teaspoon salt
1 tablespoon olive oil
1 (14.5-ounce) can cut green beans
1 (14.5-ounce) can corn
1 (15-ounce) can tomato sauce
1 (.87-ounce) packet turkey gravy mix
¾ cup ditali pasta
Salt and pepper

In a large covered saucepan, cook potatoes, carrots, and celery in 4 cups water until vegetables are tender. Meanwhile, in a large frying pan, brown turkey, onion, seasoning, and salt in oil until the turkey is no longer pink. Add turkey and all remaining ingredients, including remaining water, to the vegetables and simmer for 10–12 minutes, until the pasta is cooked. Taste and adjust seasonings.

Turkey Vegetable Soup with Dumplings

Makes 8 servings

3 tablespoons olive oil
1 pound ground turkey
1 small onion, diced
3 medium russet potatoes, diced
5 carrots, sliced
4 cups chicken broth
2 cups water
2 teaspoons salt
1/2 teaspoon pepper
16 ounces frozen peas
2 teaspoons poultry seasoning
1 teaspoon marjoram
2 (.87-ounce) envelopes chicken or turkey gravy mix
1 (16.3-ounce) can large (grande) refrigerator biscuits
2 teaspoons parsley

In a large, wide saucepan, heat oil over medium-high heat. Brown turkey and onion together, stirring frequently. Add potatoes, carrots, broth, water, salt, and pepper. Cover and bring to a boil over medium-high heat. Reduce heat to a low boil and let cook until potatoes are tender. Add peas, seasonings, and gravy packets to the soup and let simmer for 5 minutes, stirring frequently. Arrange 8 biscuits over the top and sprinkle with parsley. Cover and let simmer on low for 8–10 minutes, until biscuits are cooked.

Meat Soups

Beef Barley Soup

2 quarts broth from a boiled pot roast

1 quart water

1 quart tomatoes, chopped

2 tablespoons dehydrated onion flakes

1 cup pearl barley

1 quart green beans, drained

2 teaspoons soy sauce

2 bay leaves

3–4 cups shredded beef pot roast

2 teaspoons whole leaf thyme

3 teaspoons beef bouillon powder, divided

1/2 teaspoon pepper

Salt

Place all ingredients in a large soup pot with 2 teaspoons bouillon. Cover and bring to a boil. Reduce heat and let cook at a low boil until the barley has softened, about 45 minutes. Adjust seasonings, adding more bouillon or salt, if desired, and serve.

VARIATIONS: You can add cabbage, tomato paste, and/or carrots.

Asian-Style Broccoli Beef Soup

Makes 4 servings

2 tablespoons olive oil
1/2 pound beef steak
1 clove garlic, minced
1 teaspoon freshly grated gingerroot
1 tablespoon soy sauce
2 cups broccoli florets
1 cup finely diced jicama
2 (14.5-ounce) cans beef broth
1 handful bean sprouts

Heat oil in a deep skillet. Thinly slice the beef and stir-fry until seared and brown. Add garlic, gingerroot, and soy sauce and cook on medium-high for 1 minute. Add broccoli, jicama, and broth; cover and simmer for 8–10 minutes, until vegetables are cooked but slightly crunchy. Fold sprouts into the hot soup; cover for 1 minute.

Beef and Broccoli Soup

Makes 4 servings

2 tablespoons olive oil
1/2 pound lean beef steak, thinly sliced
1 small clove garlic, minced
1 tablespoon soy sauce
2 cups broccoli florets
2 cups water
2 teaspoons beef bouillon
1 (14.5-ounce) can Italian-style diced tomatoes

Heat oil in a deep skillet. Stir-fry beef until seared and brown. Add garlic and soy sauce and continue on medium-high for 1 minute. Add broccoli, water, and bouillon; cover and simmer for 10–15 minutes, until broccoli is tender. Pour in tomatoes, combine well, and heat through.

Vegetable Beef Stew with Gravy

Makes 8–10 *servings*

2 tablespoons olive oil

1 1/2 pounds round steak, cut into cubes and browned

2 medium onions, sliced

2 tablespoons lemon juice

2 garlic cloves, minced

3–4 quarts water, divided

3 ribs celery, sliced

8 carrots, sliced

4 potatoes, peeled, quartered, and sliced

4 ounces sliced mushrooms, optional

1 bay leaf

1 teaspoon parsley flakes

1/2 teaspoon allspice

1/2 teaspoon paprika

2 teaspoons Worcestershire sauce

1/2 cup flour mixed into 3/4 cup water

1–4 teaspoons beef bouillon powder

Salt and pepper

In a large soup pot, heat oil over medium-high heat and brown meat. Remove meat from pot and set aside. Brown onion in the meat drippings for about 2–3 minutes. Pour in lemon juice and stir to deglaze the pan. Return meat to pot, and add garlic and 1 quart water. Cover and bring to a boil; reduce heat and let meat and onion simmer for about 2 hours while the meat tenderizes.

Add vegetables, herbs, spices, Worcestershire, and enough of the remaining water to cover vegetables by 1 inch. Cover pot and bring to a boil; reduce heat to a low boil and let cook for about 30–35 minutes.

Whisk the flour and water mixture and stir it into the bubbling stew. Continue stirring for about 3 minutes while the liquid thickens. Taste the stew and season with bouillon to suit your taste; add in small portions and stir well to dissolve and distribute. Add salt and pepper, if needed.

NOTE: Inspired by a recipe for beef stew in the January 1997 *Better Homes and Gardens* magazine.

Chunky Dutch Oven Vegetable Beef Stew

Makes 8–10 *servings*

1½–2 pounds lean beef, cut in cubes

1 tablespoon Worcestershire sauce

½ (1.3-ounce) package dry onion soup and dip mix

1 medium onion, cut in chunks and layers separated

6–7 cups vegetables, cut in large chunks (carrot, celery, potato, turnip, onion, cauliflower, broccoli, bok choy, mushrooms)

1 teaspoon Italian herbs

2 teaspoons salt

1 (14.5-ounce) can tomato sauce

1 (14.5-ounce) can beef broth

1 cup water

Preheat oven to 300 degrees and spray inside of a large Dutch oven lightly with nonstick cooking spray.

Spread beef cubes over the bottom of the pan and sprinkle with Worcestershire sauce and onion soup mix. Place lid on pan and place in oven for 1 hour.

Remove pan from oven and add all the vegetables and sprinkle with herbs and salt. Pour tomato sauce, broth, and water over all. Mix vegetables and meat into the liquid. Cover, return to oven, and reduce heat to 275 degrees. Cook for 2 more hours.

Spicy Hamburger Soup

Makes 6–10 *servings*

1 pound ground beef
1 medium onion, chopped
   or 2 tablespoons
   dehydrated onion
1/4 cup chopped green
   bell pepper
1 package Chili Macaroni
   Hamburger Helper
5 cups water
1 teaspoon chile powder
1/2 teaspoon garlic salt
1/4 teaspoon salt
2 (14.5-ounce) cans
   diced tomatoes
1 (14.5-ounce) can corn,
   drained
1/2 cup sliced black
   olives, optional
Corn chips or tortilla
   chips

In a large saucepan, brown beef, onion, and bell pepper together; drain. Stir in sauce mix from the Hamburger Helper. Add water, spices, tomatoes, corn, and olives if using, and bring to a boil, stirring frequently. Reduce heat, cover, and simmer 20 minutes. Stir noodles into the soup; cover and simmer 8-10 minutes, until the noodles are soft but not mushy. Serve with chips for garnish.

Cheeseburger and Tots Soup

Makes 6–8 *servings*

1 pound lean ground
   beef
1 medium onion, chopped
1/2–3/4 cup dill relish
1 (10-ounce) can tomato
   soup, condensed
1 cup tomato sauce
1 cup ketchup
1 tablespoon prepared
   mustard
3 cups water
1 tablespoon beef base or
   2 cubes beef bouillon
Salt and pepper
6–8 thin slices cheddar
   or American cheese
1/2 (28-ounce) package
   frozen tater tots,
   baked per package
   instructions
3–4 toasted hamburger
   buns

In a large soup pot, brown beef and onion together. Add all remaining ingredients except cheese, tater tots, and buns. Mix well and heat over medium heat, stirring frequently, until soup has bubbled for 3 minutes. Serve immediately with a slice of cheese and a few tater tots garnishing each bowl. Toasted hamburger buns complete the effect.

Sesame Sirloin and Mushroom Stew

Makes 8–10 *servings*

1¹/₂ **pounds beef sirloin steak, cut into cubes ¹/₂-inch thick**

2 **tablespoons vegetable oil**

1 **large onion, roughly chopped**

2 **cloves garlic, chopped**

4 **cups water, divided**

1 **bay leaf**

1 **tablespoon beef base powder or 2 teaspoons bouillon powder**

³/₄ **cup pearl barley**

5 **large carrots, peeled and sliced**

2 **cups sliced mushrooms**

2 **tablespoons grated fresh gingerroot**

2 **cups bok choy, chopped, white and green parts**

1 **tablespoon soy sauce**

¹/₂ **teaspoon sesame oil**

Sesame seeds

In a large soup pot, brown the beef cubes in hot oil over medium-high heat, turning occasionally. Keep the heat high enough that the meat browns without losing its juices. Add the onion and garlic and continue browning for about 3 minutes. Pour in 1 cup water and loosen the brown bits from bottom of the pan, then add remainder of the water and bay leaf. Cover and reduce heat to a vigorous simmer for about 1¹/₂ hours.

When meat is fork-tender, add the barley, carrots, mushrooms, and gingerroot and cook for 30 minutes. As the barley absorbs the liquid, add 1–2 cups more water, if needed. About 25 minutes before serving, add the bok choy and soy sauce. When the bok choy is tender, drizzle in sesame oil and stir. Taste the soup and adjust seasonings with bouillon and soy sauce, adding just a little at a time until it pleases your palate. Garnish each bowl with a tiny sprinkling of sesame seeds.

Beefy Tomato Rotini Soup

Makes 6–8 servings

1 pound ground beef
1 medium onion, diced
1 pound rotini pasta,
    cooked al dente and
    drained
2 (14.5-ounce) cans
    Italian-style diced
    tomatoes
2 cups V-8 juice
2 cups water
2 beef bouillon cubes
2 teaspoons sugar
Salt and pepper

In a large saucepan, brown ground beef and onion together; drain off and discard grease.

Combine all remaining ingredients with the beef and onion and bring to a light boil; let simmer for 5 minutes, stirring frequently, while the bouillon cubes dissolve and flavors meld. Season to taste with salt and pepper.

Stroganoff Noodle Soup

1 pound sirloin beef
  steak
2 tablespoons vegetable
  oil
8 ounces sliced
  mushrooms
2 1/2 cups beef broth
2 tablespoons butter
2 tablespoons flour
1/2 cup sour cream
1 1/2 cups milk
1/2 teaspoon paprika
1/4 teaspoon pepper
Salt
1/2 pound fettuccine,
  cooked

Slice the beef across the grain into thin strips then cut into 1-inch lengths. In a deep skillet or a saucepan, brown meat in oil, stirring frequently. Add mushrooms and toss with meat; continue cooking until meat and mushrooms are cooked through. Add broth.

In a small saucepan, melt butter and stir in the flour; cook for 4 minutes to make a roux. Stir sour cream into the roux and then whisk in the milk. Add roux to the beef with broth and whisk together to make a sauce. Add paprika, pepper, and salt, to taste. Stir noodles into the soup and coat. Heat through and serve.

Taco Soup

Makes 8–10 *servings*

1½ pounds ground beef
1 medium onion, diced
2 (14.5-ounce) cans
　　kidney beans,
　　drained and rinsed
2 (14.5-ounce) cans
　　diced tomatoes
2 (14.5-ounce) cans
　　corn, drained
2 (14.5-ounce) cans beef
　　broth
1 tablespoon chile pow-
　　der or 1 tablespoon
　　diced jalapeno chiles
Garnishes: crumbled
　　Mexican cheese such
　　as cotija, sour cream,
　　guacamole, corn chips

Brown beef and onion together in a large frying pan; drain grease. Place all ingredients in a large soup pot; cover and bring to a boil, stirring frequently. Reduce heat and simmer for about 15 minutes. Ladle into bowls and garnish as desired.

VARIATION: You can substitute chicken and chicken broth for the beef. Be sure the chicken is well cooked before adding to the soup pot.

Dutch Oven Mushroom Beef Soup with Gnocchi

Makes 6–8 *servings*

2 tablespoons olive oil

1 pound beef chunks, trimmed

8 ounces mushrooms, quartered

1 medium onion, cut in wedges

2 Knorr beef bouillon cubes

4 cups water

1 sprig fresh rosemary

Salt and pepper

1 cup cream

1 pound gnocchi, cooked in water per package directions

Preheat oven to 200 degrees.

Heat olive oil in a Dutch oven and brown beef on at least two sides. Place all ingredients, except cream and gnocchi, in the pan. Cook, covered, in oven for 4 hours, or until meat is tender. Remove from oven and stir in cream; adjust seasoning with salt and pepper, if needed. Return soup to oven for 30 minutes, if needed, to reheat. To serve, divide gnocchi into soup bowls and spoon the beef soup over the top.

Beef Stew with Noodles

Makes 8 servings

1 1/2 pound beef chunks, trimmed

2 tablespoons olive oil

1 large onion, cut in wedges

2 cloves garlic, minced

8 ounces sliced mushrooms

5 carrots, peeled and sliced

3 Knorr beef bouillon cubes

6 cups water

1 teaspoon Worcestershire sauce

1 teaspoon soy sauce

1 bunch Italian parsley, chopped

1 (10.5-ounce) can cream of mushroom soup, condensed

1/2 cup milk or half-and-half

2 cups home-style noodles

Preheat oven to 200 degrees.

In a large Dutch oven, brown beef in hot oil. Add all remaining ingredients except milk and noodles. Cover pan and cook in oven for 4 hours. Remove from oven and stir in milk and noodles. Cover and return to oven for 1 hour to cook the noodles.

Florene's Coleslaw Soup

Makes 6–8 servings

1 pound ground beef
2 medium potatoes,
    peeled and diced
2 teaspoons dehydrated
    onion flakes
1 (13-ounce) package
    prepared coleslaw
2 beef bouillon cubes
3 cups water
Pepper

In a medium saucepan, brown the ground beef. Add all ingredients except pepper. Cover and bring to a boil; reduce heat to a low boil for about 30 minutes. Taste and adjust flavor with pepper or a small addition of bouillon.

Danish Chop Suey

Makes 4–6 servings

5–6 slices bacon,
    chopped
1 small onion, chopped
1 pound ground beef
1 (14.5-ounce) can
    stewed tomatoes
1 cup tomato juice
1 (14.5-ounce) can
    kidney beans,
    drained and rinsed
1 cup chopped celery
3–4 cups cooked rice

In a large frying pan, brown bacon and onion together; drain and transfer to a medium soup pot. In the same frying pan, brown ground beef; drain and transfer to pot. Add all remaining ingredients except rice. Cover pot and simmer on low heat until celery is cooked. Serve over rice.

NOTE: We think this recipe originated in the 1930s on the East Coast. No one knows how the name came about.

Hearty Meatball Soup with Pasta

1 small onion, chopped
2 carrots, diced
1 tablespoon olive oil
4 cups water
2 large or 4 small beef
   bouillon cubes
1 (28-ounce) can or jar
   spaghetti sauce, of
   choice
1 (1.45-ounce) can corn,
   drained
1/2 teaspoon oregano
1 pound frozen
   meatballs
2 cups elbow or shell
   macaroni
1/2 cup grated Parmesan
   or Asiago cheese

In a large saucepan, saute onion and carrots in hot oil for 5 minutes. Add water and bouillon and bring to a boil; reduce heat to simmer for 10 minutes. Add all remaining ingredients except cheese. Be sure pasta is stirred into the soup. Cover pot and bring to a simmer, stirring frequently, for 20–25 minutes, until pasta is cooked al dente. Serve with a sprinkling of cheese.

Slow Pot Roast Stew

Makes 6–8 *servings*

2 tablespoons olive oil

1 (2-pound) boneless
    beef chuck roast,
    fat trimmed

Salt

1 medium onion, cut in
    wedges

1 pound mini carrots

3 large baking potatoes,
    thickly sliced

3 cups water

Add oil to a medium frying pan over medium-high heat and brown the roast on both sides. Transfer meat to a 3½-quart or larger slow cooker. Salt the meat then layer in the onion, carrots, and potatoes. Lightly salt the vegetables and add water. Cook on low for 8–10 hours, or on high for 3 hours then on low for about 2 hours. Serve vegetables and meat in bowls with broth ladled over top.

Ham and Corn Chowder

Makes 8 servings

3 medium russet
  potatoes, peeled
  and diced
1 cup chopped onion
1 stalks celery, diced
3 cups water
2 rounded teaspoons
  chicken bouillon
  powder
1 cup diced cooked ham
2 (15-ounce) cans corn,
  drained
3 tablespoons butter
4 tablespoons flour
1 cup half-and-half
1/4 teaspoon pepper

In a medium soup pot, boil potato, onion, and celery in water about 25 minutes, until vegetables are tender. Add bouillon, ham, and corn and heat through.

Make a white sauce by cooking butter and flour together in a small frying pan for 3 minutes then whisk the half-and-half into the flour mixture a little at a time until it is thin enough to pour. Stir white sauce into the soup until well incorporated and stir in pepper. Add remaining half-and-half to thin the soup, if desired. Heat through and serve.

Minestrone with Sweet Potato and Ham

Makes 8 servings

1 medium onion, chopped
1 cup sliced celery
2 tablespoons olive oil
3 cups thinly sliced
  cabbage
3 cups cubed sweet
  potato
3 cups diced cooked ham
2 (14.5-ounce) cans
  Italian-style tomatoes
2 (15-ounce) cans cut
  green beans, drained
1 (15-ounce) can
  cannellini beans,
  drained
4 cups chicken broth
Hot water to cover
  vegetables
1 teaspoon each dried
  basil, oregano, whole
  thyme
$1/2$ teaspoon garlic
  powder
$1^1/2$ teaspoons sugar
2 small zucchini, halved
  and sliced
Salt and pepper

In a large soup pot, saute onion and celery in hot oil. Add all remaining ingredients except zucchini and salt and pepper. Cover and bring to a boil over high heat, stirring frequently; reduce to a low boil for about 30 minutes to cook raw vegetables and meld flavors. Add zucchini during last 10 minutes of cooking. Taste and adjust seasonings with salt and pepper.

Hambone Soup

Makes 10 servings

1 pound dried white
  beans
1 ham bone with meat
1–2 cups chopped ham
1 large onion, chopped
5 ribs celery, chopped
6–8 carrots, chopped
1 bay leaf
8–10 cups water
2 tablespoons ham base
1/2 teaspoon pepper
Salt

Soak and prepare beans for cooking according to package directions. Place all ingredients except salt in a large soup pot. Cover and bring to a boil, then reduce heat and simmer soup for 2½–4 hours, until beans are soft. Taste and adjust seasonings with salt, if needed. Alternatively, cook in a large slow cooker on low heat for 8–10 hours.

Slow Posole

Makes 6–8 servings

1 tablespoon vegetable
  oil
1 pound lean pork, cubed
1 cup chopped onion
1 (14-ounce) can mild
  red enchilada sauce
1 (24-ounce) can white
  hominy, drained
1 teaspoon oregano
2–3 cups sliced cabbage
1/2 teaspoon cumin
1/2 teaspoon chile powder
2 teaspoons salt

Pour oil into a 3-quart or larger slow cooker and add the pork, onion, and enchilada sauce; mix together. Add all remaining ingredients and cook on low for 8 hours or on high for 3–3½ hours, until hominy begins to split and cabbage is cooked.

Chinese Pork Noodle Soup

Makes 4–6 *servings*

1 pound lean pork, cubed

1 cup diced yellow onion

2 tablespoons vegetable oil

2 scallions, sliced, white and green parts

1 large clove garlic, minced

1 cup sliced celery

2 (14.5-ounce) cans chicken broth

2 teaspoons rice vinegar

1 (8-ounce) can bamboo shoots, drained and cut in half lengthwise

2 cups fresh bean sprouts

$1/2$ teaspoon ground ginger

8 ounces rice noodles, cooked in water per package directions

In a medium saucepan, brown pork and onion in hot oil. (Use a splatter guard to prevent grease burns; a lid will cause the pork to steam instead of brown.) Add scallions, garlic, celery, broth, and vinegar; cover pot and simmer for about 30 minutes, until pork is tender. Add bamboo and heat through. Stir in sprouts and ginger. Add cooked noodles and stir into the liquid. Heat through and serve.

Teriyaki Pork Soup

Makes 6 *servings*

1 pound thick, lean,
  boneless pork
  chops, trimmed and
  marinated*
2 tablespoons vegetable
  oil
2 cups cubed sweet
  potato
1/3 cup sliced green
  onions
1 small clove garlic,
  minced
1/2 cup diced red bell
  pepper
4–8 ounces mushrooms,
  sliced
1 cup water
2 (14.5-ounce) cans
  chicken broth
2 tablespoons teriyaki
  sauce
1 teaspoon grated fresh
  gingerroot
1 (15-ounce) package
  Chinese noodles,
  broken into thirds

After pork has marinated, slice it very thinly and stir-fry in a medium frying pan on medium-high heat until cooked through. Combine all ingredients except noodles in a medium saucepan; cover and simmer until potatoes are tender, about 12 minutes. Add noodles and stir well; cover pan and cook the noodles.

*Marinate pork lightly in purchased teriyaki sauce for several hours.

Pork and Greens

1½ pounds mild sweet Italian ground pork sausage

½ cup chopped onion

1 small zucchini, sliced

1 bunch kale, tough stems removed

1 bunch collards, stems trimmed

3 chicken bouillon cubes

¼ teaspoon Cajun seasoning

3 cups water

3 cups packed spinach leaves

½ pint whipping cream

1 cup acini de pepi, cooked and drained

In a large frying pan, brown the sausage with onion; drain and discard the fat; set aside.

In a large saucepan, boil zucchini, kale, collards, bouillon, and seasoning in the water about 8–10 minutes, until greens are fork-tender. Remove from heat. Add spinach and push it under the water so it wilts. Puree about 2 cups of greens with the cream then return to the pot. Add the sausage and pasta; stir well. Taste and adjust seasonings.

Italian Sausage and Lasagna Soup

Makes 8 *servings*

1/2 pound ground Italian
sausage,* browned
and drained
1 (26-ounce) can
spaghetti sauce
with vegetables
3 cups vegetable broth
3/4 part-skim ricotta
cheese
1 (10-ounce) box frozen
chopped spinach
1 (15-ounce) can
cannellini beans,
optional
1/4 teaspoon garlic
powder
1 teaspoon Italian herbs
2 teaspoons beef base
powder
2 tablespoons dehy-
drated onion flakes
4–5 lasagna noodles,
broken into pieces
Grated Parmesan
cheese, optional

Place all ingredients into a slow
cooker, in order given, and cook on
low for 4–8 hours. (Hold noodles
until the last 1–2 hours of cooking if
you like them al dente.) Stir twice
during cooking to mix the ingredients. Serve sprinkled with cheese.

*Pork or turkey

Chinese Pork Meatball Soup

Makes 4–6 servings

Meatballs

1/2 pound ground pork
3/4 cup bread crumbs
1 teaspoon soy sauce
1 teaspoon cornstarch
2 scallions, thinly
    sliced, white and
    green parts
1 teaspoon grated fresh
    gingerroot
1 egg

Soup

2 (14.5-ounce) cans
    chicken broth
1/2 cup water
1 whole clove garlic
1 teaspoon teriyaki sauce
2 cups shredded Napa
    cabbage
1 cup bean sprouts
Salt

In a medium bowl, using your hands, mix meatball ingredients together until well blended.

Bring broth, water, garlic, and teriyaki sauce to a boil in a large saucepan. Form teaspoon-size meatballs and lower into the boiling broth as you go. When all meatballs are in, cover and reduce to a simmer for 50–60 minutes while pork cooks through. Add vegetables to soup, cover, and boil for 3–5 minutes. Season to taste with salt.

Italian Meatball and Pasta Soup

Makes 4–6 *servings*

Meatballs
1/2 **pound ground pork**
3/4 **cup seasoned Italian bread crumbs**
1/4 **cup grated Parmesan cheese**
1 teaspoon cornstarch
2 scallions, finely chopped, white and green parts
1 egg

Soup
1 medium onion, finely chopped
2 cloves garlic, minced
1 cup grated carrots
2 ribs celery, finely chopped
2 Knorr chicken bouillon cubes
1 teaspoon dried red chile flakes
1 teaspoon Italian seasoning
1/2 **teaspoon paprika**
10 cups water
1 cup small tube pasta (such as ditalini)
Salt

Pulse meatball ingredients in a food processor a few times; turn into a bowl and finish mixing by hand; refrigerate.

In a large soup pot, bring soup ingredients, except pasta and salt, to a boil. Retrieve meat mixture and shape teaspoon-size meatballs. Drop them gently into the boiling soup. Cover and simmer for 40 minutes. Add pasta and boil gently for 7–8 minutes, or until pasta is al dente. Season to taste with salt.

Lit'l Smokies and Cabbage Stew

Makes 6–8 *servings*

1 medium onion, chopped
1/2 cup chopped red bell
    pepper
1 tablespoon olive oil
4 cups roughly chopped
    cabbage
4 carrots, peeled and
    sliced
2 ribs celery, sliced
1 pound Lit'l Smokies
    sausages
1 (14.5-ounce) can red
    or white beans,
    drained and rinsed
1 (14.5-ounce) can
    stewed tomatoes
1 (6-ounce) can tomato
    paste
1 bay leaf
1/2 teaspoon marjoram
3/4 cup uncooked long-
    grain rice
2 large beef bouillon
    cubes
1 large chicken bouillon
    cube
8 cups water

In a large saucepan, saute onion and bell pepper in hot oil until onion turns translucent. Add all other ingredients to the pan. Cover and bring to a boil; reduce heat, and simmer for 45– 60 minutes, until vegetables are cooked.

Cabbage and Brats Soup

Makes 6–8 *servings*

2 tablespoons olive oil

1 medium onion,
    roughly chopped

6 smoked Bratwurst
    sausages, casing
    removed, sliced in
    rounds

4–5 cups cubed potatoes

1 small head cabbage,
    cored and roughly
    chopped

1 (14.5-ounce) can beef
    broth

1 (14.5-ounce) can
    chicken broth

Water

1 tablespoon Dijon
    mustard

1 teaspoon Worcester-
    shire sauce

1 bay leaf

$1/2$ teaspoon paprika

$1/4$ teaspoon whole thyme

$1/4$ teaspoon marjoram

Generous pinch red
    chile flakes

Small pinch ground
    cloves

Salt and pepper

In a large saucepan, heat oil on medium high and saute onion for 2 minutes. Add sausage and saute 2–3 minutes more, stirring. Add all remaining ingredients and stir to combine. Cover and bring to a boil over high heat, stirring frequently. Reduce to medium and cook at a low boil for 20–25 minutes, stirring frequently, until vegetables are tender. Let simmer 5 extra minutes. Taste and adjust seasonings.

Fish & Seafood
Stews, Soups,
& Chowders

Fisherman's Stew

Makes 6–8 servings

2 tablespoons olive oil
1 medium onion, chopped
3 ribs celery, finely
  diced
3–4 carrots, diced
3 medium potatoes,
  peeled and diced
1 bay leaf
1 teaspoon oregano or
  thyme
2 (14.5-ounce) cans
  chicken broth
2 (14.5-ounce) cans
  diced tomatoes,
  with liquid
4–6 tablespoons cocktail
  sauce
1/4 teaspoon Creole
  seasoning
1/2 pound frozen shrimp
  (31–40 count), thawed
8 ounces frozen bay
  scallops
4 cups cooked rice

In a large saucepan, heat oil on medium high and saute onion, celery, and carrots together for about 10 minutes, until they begin to soften. Add potatoes, herbs, and broth; cover pan and bring to a boil to finish cooking vegetables, about 10 minutes. Add tomatoes, sauce, and Creole seasoning. Bring to a boil once again then add seafood and heat for 5–10 minutes. Taste and adjust seasonings. Serve in bowls over cooked rice.

Catfish Stew

Makes 10–12 *servings*

2 tablespoons olive oil
1 medium onion, chopped
3 ribs celery, thinly
  sliced
3 medium carrots, diced
1 (14.5-ounce) can
  chicken broth
3 cups water, divided
1 (19-ounce) jar red
  peppers, drained
  and chopped
1 quart stewed tomatoes
  or 2 (14.5-ounce)
  cans diced tomatoes
1–2 teaspoons Cajun
  seasoning
1¹/₂ large frozen catfish
  fillets
Salt and pepper
5–6 cups cooked rice

In a large saucepan, heat oil over medium-high heat and saute onion and celery until they begin to soften. Add carrots and broth, plus enough water to just cover. Cover pan and bring to a boil; cook until vegetables are soft, 20–25 minutes. Add peppers, tomatoes, and seasoning and bring to a boil. Lay the catfish fillets on top and press them into the soup until they're submerged. Cover pan and simmer 20–25 minutes, until catfish is cooked. Test doneness with a fork; when the thickest part of the fish flakes, it's done. Transfer fish to a cutting board and cut or break into small pieces, then return to the pan. Reheat and taste for seasonings. Serve in bowls over rice.

Manhattan Clam Chowder

Makes 6–8 *servings*

2 strips bacon, cut in
   small pieces
1/3 cup chopped onion
1/4 cup chopped green
   bell pepper
1 rib celery, chopped
5 cups water
Bouquet garni tied in
   cheesecloth (1 bay
   leaf, 3–4 whole
   cloves, 1 whole carda-
   mom, 1 clove garlic)
1/2 teaspoon whole
   thyme leaves
1/4 teaspoon freshly
   ground pepper
2 carrots, diced
3 medium potatoes, diced
2 Roma tomatoes, diced
2 (6.5-ounce) cans
   minced clams, with
   liquid
2 tablespoons butter
2 tablespoons flour
   dissolved in 2
   tablespoons water
Salt

In a medium saucepan, cook the bacon over medium heat until crispy. Add onion, bell pepper, and celery; saute until onion begins to turn translucent, stirring frequently. Add water, bouquet garni, thyme, pepper, vegetables, tomatoes, and liquid from the canned clams to the pot. Cover and bring to a boil, then reduce heat and simmer for 30 minutes, or until vegetables are tender.

Meanwhile, in a small frying pan, saute clams in butter for 2 minutes, but do not let them brown. Stir flour mixture into the clams until well incorporated; turn off heat. When vegetables are cooked, remove the bouquet garni then add clams to the soup, stirring briskly to prevent flour lumps. Continue stirring until the soup thickens. Adjust seasoning with salt.

New England
Clam Chowder

Makes 10–12 *servings*

2 pounds russet potatoes, peeled and diced

5 stalks celery, finely diced

1/2 small onion, finely diced

1/2 cup diced green bell pepper

1 large leek, diced, white and green parts

2 tablespoons red wine vinegar

2 bay leaves

1/2 teaspoon whole leaf thyme

2 teaspoons salt

1/2 teaspoon pepper

Water

1 stick butter

10 tablespoons flour

3 cups half-and-half, divided

2 (6-ounce) cans chopped clams, with liquid

2–3 shakes hot sauce of choice

Place all the vegetables, vinegar, herbs, salt, and pepper in a large soup pot and cover with water. Cover pot with a lid and bring to a boil; reduce heat to a low boil and cook about 25 minutes, until vegetables are tender.

Meanwhile, make roux by cooking butter and flour together in a small frying pan for 3–4 minutes. Stir frequently to avoid burning. Thin the roux with 1/4-cup additions of hot soup liquid until it becomes like thick paste.

When vegetables are cooked, pour in 2 cups half-and-half and clams. Stir well. Using a sturdy whisk, thicken soup with the roux. If soup is too thick, add remaining half-and-half. Shake in hot sauce and mix well. Heat through. Taste and adjust seasonings.

Canned Salmon Chowder

Makes 10–12 servings

4 slices bacon, chopped
1 cup chopped onion
1 cup sliced celery
1 green bell pepper, diced
1 teaspoon paprika
1 tablespoon vegetable oil
1 tablespoon butter
4 rounded tablespoons flour
2 large potatoes, cut in small dice
1 cup water
2 cups milk, divided
1 cup whipping cream
1 (14.75-ounce) can pink or red salmon, drained and deboned
2 tablespoons lemon juice
2 teaspoons salt
$^1/_2$ teaspoon pepper

In a large saucepan over medium heat, saute bacon, onion, celery, bell pepper, and paprika in hot oil, stirring frequently, until bacon begins to cook, about 10 minutes. Add butter and sprinkle in the flour; continue cooking for 3–4 minutes. Add potatoes, water, and 1 cup milk to saucepan and stir well. Heat to boiling, stirring frequently, as liquid thickens. Reduce heat, cover pan, and simmer 25 minutes, or until potatoes are tender, stirring frequently. When potatoes are cooked, add rest of milk and all remaining ingredients. Stir well and simmer until heated through.

Snapper Chowder

Makes 6–8 *servings*

- 4 medium potatoes, diced
- 1 small sprig rosemary
- Water
- 1 cup chopped green and kalamata olives
- 1/2 cup chopped marinated artichoke hearts
- 1 yellow bell pepper, diced
- 4 tablespoons butter
- 4 red snapper fillets, coated in flour
- 1/2 lemon, juiced
- 2 tablespoons dehydrated onion flakes
- 2 cubes vegetable bouillon
- 1 teaspoon Old Bay seasoning
- 2 cups seafood stock
- 2 cups chicken broth
- 1 cup whipping cream
- 1 teaspoon hot sauce
- 2 tablespoons flour mixed with 2 tablespoons soft butter
- Salt and pepper

In a medium saucepan, boil potatoes and rosemary in just enough water to cover; when fork tender, drain and discard rosemary.

Meanwhile, in a large saucepan, saute olives, artichoke, and bell pepper in butter for 3–4 minutes; remove from pan and set aside. Cook fillets in the same pan, 4 minutes per side. Sprinkle with lemon juice during cooking. Break up fish and add all recipe ingredients to the pan. Bring to a light boil over medium-high heat, whisking, until the flour incorporates and the liquid thickens. Adjust seasonings.

Easy Salad Shrimp Bisque

Makes 4–6 *servings*

1/2 cup chopped onion
1 tablespoon olive oil
1 tablespoon plus
   2 teaspoons butter,
   divided
1/2 teaspoon whole
   thyme leaves
1/4 teaspoon ground bay
   leaf
1/8 teaspoon garlic
   powder
1 cup water
1 cup mashed potato
   flakes
1/2 cup whipping cream
2 cups milk
2 cups cooked salad
   shrimp, thawed
Salt and pepper

In a small saucepan, saute onion in oil and 1 tablespoon butter for about 4 minutes, until onion turns translucent. Add the herbs and garlic while cooking.

In a medium saucepan over medium-high heat, bring water and remaining butter to a boil. Add potato flakes and stir in. Reduce heat to low and add cream and milk. If bisque is too thin, sprinkle in more potato flakes; if too thick, add more milk. When soup is the consistency you like, stir in the shrimp and let soup simmer for 3–5 minutes, stirring frequently. Adjust seasoning with salt and pepper.

Shrimp Creole Soup

Makes 8–10 servings

2 cups chopped celery
2 bunches green onions, chopped
2–4 cloves garlic, minced
2 tablespoons olive oil
3 (14.5-ounce) cans chicken broth
2 (14.5 ounce) cans diced tomatoes
1/2 teaspoon sugar
1/4 teaspoon dried thyme
1/4 teaspoon pepper
1 cup instant rice
1 1/2–2 pounds green shrimp, shelled and deveined
Salt
Hot sauce, of choice

Lightly saute vegetables and garlic in oil. Add broth, tomatoes, sugar, and spices. Simmer for 20–30 minutes. Then add rice and simmer until tender. Add the shrimp just minutes before you are ready to eat. As soon as they are all pink, season with salt and hot sauce and eat it up. Yum!

Crab Bisque

Makes 4–6 servings

1 tablespoon butter
1 tablespoon flour
2 cups milk
1/2 teaspoon salt
1 teaspoon minced fresh parsley
4 cups fish stock
2 cups minced crabmeat
1 tablespoon lemon juice
1/2–3/4 cup fine breadcrumbs, to taste
Dash hot sauce, optional

In a medium saucepan, melt butter over medium heat and stir in flour. Very slowly add milk, whisking constantly to form a lump-free white sauce; do not let it boil. When milk is all incorporated, add salt, parsley, stock, crabmeat, lemon juice, and breadcrumbs. Heat through. Taste and adjust seasoning with salt and hot sauce, if desired.

Smoked Herring Soup

1 tablespoon butter

1/2 small onion, finely diced

1 rib celery, finely diced

1 tablespoon finely chopped green bell pepper

1 small potato, diced

1 cup water

1/2 teaspoon dill weed

1 teaspoon lemon juice

2 cups milk

Salt and pepper

1 (3.25-ounce) tin boneless smoked herring fillets, chopped*

In a medium saucepan, heat butter and saute onion, celery, and bell pepper 3–4 minutes, to give it a head start. Add all other ingredients, except herring, and bring to a low boil; reduce to a simmer and cook 20–30 minutes. Add herring and simmer 5 minutes more. Adjust seasoning with salt and pepper.

*Remove the fish skin before chopping, if you wish.

Grilled Salmon Chowder

Makes 6–8 servings

1 pound salmon fillet
$\frac{1}{2}$ teaspoon salt
1 teaspoon dill weed
Juice of 2 lemons,
    divided
3 tablespoons olive oil
2 tablespoons butter
1 small onion, diced
1 leek, cleaned and diced
1 clove garlic, minced
1 green bell pepper,
    diced
1 red bell pepper, diced
$\frac{1}{2}$ cup flour
2 medium russet
    potatoes, peeled
    and finely diced
2 (14.5-ounce) cans
    chicken broth
1 cup whipping cream
1 cup milk

Grill the salmon just until you can flake it with a fork; it can be slightly underdone in the center as it will continue to cook in the soup. Sprinkle salt, dill, and 2 tablespoons lemon juice over flesh side as it cooks. Transfer fish to a plate and remove the skin. Flake the fish into small bite-size pieces. Set aside.

In a large saucepan, heat the oil and butter over medium heat; saute onion, leek, and garlic about 5 minutes, stirring frequently. Add bell peppers and saute 3–5 minutes more then stir in the flour. Add potatoes and broth. Stir all together, and bring to a boil over medium-high heat. Reduce heat and simmer potatoes about 12 minutes, until tender, stirring to prevent sticking. Add salmon, cream, milk, and remaining lemon juice. Let simmer for about 5 minutes, stirring frequently.

Shrimp Curry

3 tablespoons olive oil
1 medium onion, cut
    in thin wedges and
    separated
2 cloves garlic, finely
    minced
1/2 cup diced green bell
    pepper
2 cups chopped carrots
2 (14.5-ounce) cans
    diced tomatoes
2 cups fish stock
1 cup water
1 tablespoon Asian fish
    sauce
1/2 teaspoon masala
    blend spice
2 teaspoons curry
    powder
1 teaspoon sugar
1 teaspoon salt
Pepper
3/4 pound green shrimp,
    peeled and deveined*
1/3 cup uncooked
    couscous

In a large saucepan, heat oil over medium heat. Saute onion, garlic, and bell pepper for about 5 minutes, until onion begins to turn translucent. Add all remaining ingredients, except shrimp and couscous. Cover and bring to a low boil and cook over medium heat for 10 minutes. Add shrimp and couscous and stir into the soup. Bring to a low boil for another 10 minutes. Taste and adjust seasonings, if needed, or with water if tomato flavor is too prominent.

*Cooked shrimp can be substituted. Provide 6–8 shrimps per serving.

Cajun Shrimp Gumbo

Makes 6–8 servings

4 cups chicken broth
1 cup water
1 medium onion, chopped
3 stalks celery, sliced
1 green bell pepper,
    diced
5 plum tomatoes, peeled,
    seeded, and chopped
1 cup frozen sliced okra
3/4 cup uncooked long
    grain white rice
1 teaspoon Old Bay
    seasoning
1 teaspoon Cajun
    seasoning
2 teaspoons salt
1 tablespoon cornstarch
    mixed into 2 table-
    spoons cold water
1 pound raw shrimp,
    shelled and deveined
Hot sauce, optional

Place all ingredients except corn-starch mixture, shrimp, and hot sauce in a large saucepan. Stir together and bring to a boil over medium-high heat. Reduce heat and simmer for about 35 minutes, or until rice is cooked. Thicken liquid with cornstarch mixture. Add shrimp and push under the liquid. Continue at a low boil just until shrimp turn pink all over. Taste and adjust seasonings; add a few drops of hot sauce, if desired.

Cheesy Tuna Chowder

Makes 4 servings

1 small onion, chopped

1 rib celery, chopped

1/4 teaspoon whole leaf thyme

1/2 teaspoon dill weed

2 medium potatoes, diced

4 tablespoons butter

1/2 cup water

2 tablespoons flour

3 cups milk

1 (8-ounce) can tomato sauce

1 (5-ounce) can tuna, drained

1 cup grated Monterey Jack cheese

2 teaspoons chopped fresh parsley

Spray bottom of a medium saucepan with nonstick cooking spray. Saute onion, celery, herbs, and potato in butter over medium heat for about 10 minutes. Add water and cover; simmer over medium-low heat until potato is tender, stirring occasionally to prevent sticking. Whisk flour into milk. Pour milk and tomato sauce into the potatoes. Add tuna. Bring to a low boil over medium heat. Stir in cheese until it has melted. Serve with a parsley garnish.

Yakisoba with Crab

Makes 4 servings

2 (7.5-ounce) packages
   yakisoba noodles*
2 tablespoons vegetable
   oil
½ cup sliced green
   onion or leek
½ cup matchstick-
   sliced red bell pepper
1 cup thinly sliced
   carrot
1 cup diagonally sliced
   sugar snap peas
1 cup shredded Napa
   cabbage
1½ teaspoons soy sauce
2 teaspoons Asian fish
   sauce
1¼ cups water
1 (13.5-ounce) can
   coconut milk
1½–2 cups imitation
   crabmeat, flaked

Open yakisoba noodles and loosen per package directions; set aside.

In a large deep skillet, heat the oil then stir-fry the onion, bell pepper, and carrot for 2–3 minutes. Add peas, cabbage, sauces, and noodles, and stir-fry for 1–2 additional minutes. Pour in water, coconut milk, and crab; heat through. Taste and adjust seasonings.

*Often found in the refrigerated produce section of the supermarket.

Cheesy Crab Soup

Makes 4–6 servings

1 small leek, washed
    and chopped, white
    and green parts
2 ribs celery, diced
1/2 red bell pepper, diced
1 large carrot, diced
1 tablespoon olive oil
1 tablespoon butter
1 (14.5-ounce) can
    vegetable broth
1 1/4 cups milk or
    half-and-half
1/4 teaspoon paprika
Salt and pepper
1 tablespoon cornstarch
    mixed with 2
    tablespoons water
1 cup grated cheddar
    jack cheese
1 cup frozen peas
3 ounces imitation
    crabmeat, cut
    bite-size

In a medium saucepan, cover and saute vegetables in oil and butter over medium heat for 15 minutes, until vegetables are tender. Stir frequently. Add broth, milk, seasonings, and cornstarch mixture and bring to a boil for 1 minute over medium-high heat, stirring constantly. Add cheese and stir until melted. Add peas and crab and reduce heat to medium; let simmer, stirring, while peas thaw and crab heats through. Taste and adjust seasonings.

Halibut Au Gratin Soup

Makes 4 servings

1 tablespoon butter
1 tablespoon flour
3 cups milk, divided
1¼ cups grated cheddar
   cheese, divided
2 cups fish stock
Salt and pepper
2 large russet potatoes,
   peeled and thinly
   sliced
12–16 ounces halibut
   fillets, cut in ½-inch
   pieces*

Preheat oven to 350 degrees and prepare a 6-quart casserole dish with nonstick cooking spray.

In a small saucepan over medium heat, cook the butter and flour together for 1 minute. Slowly add 1 cup milk, whisking constantly to make a smooth white sauce. Add 1 cup cheese and stir to melt. Gradually add remaining milk and stock. Taste and season with salt and pepper.

Layer potatoes into the baking dish and arrange halibut on top. Cover completely with the white sauce. Sprinkle with remaining cheese. Bake, covered, for 40 minutes or until potatoes are tender. Ladle into bowls and serve.

*Can be frozen; if so, bake 5–7 minutes longer.

Bean, Pea, & Lentil Soups

Lima Bean 'n' Ham Soup

Makes 10–12 *servings*

1 (16-ounce) bag dried
   baby lima beans
6 cups water for soaking
1 large onion, diced
3 ribs celery, diced
   small
5 carrots, peeled and
   diced small
2 (14.5-ounce) cans
   chicken broth
3 cups finely diced ham
Water
Salt and pepper
3–4 slices bacon, finely
   chopped and cooked
   crisp

Soak beans 8 hours or overnight in cold water. Drain and discard water.

Place all the ingredients, except salt and pepper and bacon, in a 5- to 6-quart slow cooker. Add enough water to cover. Cook 6–8 hours or more on low, until the beans are cooked to your liking. Taste the broth and adjust flavor with salt and pepper. Garnish with crumbled bacon.

Red Lentil and Barley Soup

Makes 8–10 *servings*

3 tablespoons olive oil
1 large onion, diced
4 ribs celery, thinly
    sliced
5–6 carrots, sliced
1 medium sweet potato,
    diced
1 cup pearl barley
1½ cups dried red lentils
4 cups chicken broth
6 cups water
4 cubes Knorr vegetable
    bouillon
1½ teaspoons cumin
½ teaspoon ground
    cloves
2 teaspoons oregano
½ teaspoon whole leaf
    thyme
2 teaspoons salt
1 teaspoon pepper
½ teaspoon garlic
    powder
½ small head cabbage,
    thinly sliced
1 (6-ounce) can tomato
    paste, optional

In a large saucepan, heat oil over medium-high heat. Saute onion, celery, and carrots in the hot oil, stirring frequently, until onion turns translucent. Add all other ingredients except cabbage and tomato paste, and bring to a boil. Cover and cook for about 45 minutes, stirring frequently to avoid sticking, until the barley has absorbed liquid and expanded. Add more water during cooking, if needed, to cover grains and vegetables by about 2 inches. Taste for seasonings and adjust, adding more bouillon or other seasonings to suit your taste.* When the barley is done, add the cabbage and let cook for about 8 minutes more. Stir in tomato paste, if using.

*Cumin can overpower all other flavors, so be cautious when adding more.

Fiery Lentil Soup {V}

Makes 6–8 *servings*

1 medium onion, chopped
2 tablespoons vegetable
   oil
2 cloves garlic, minced
1 (32-ounce) box
   vegetable broth
3/4 cup dried lentils,
   rinsed
2 (10-ounce) cans
   tomatoes with
   diced chiles
1 (15-ounce) can kidney
   beans, drained and
   rinsed
1 tablespoon cumin
1 teaspoon oregano
1 tablespoon chile
   powder

In a medium saucepan, brown onion in oil; add garlic the last couple minutes of cooking. Pour broth and lentils into the pan and bring to a boil; reduce heat and simmer about 30 minutes, until lentils are soft. Add all remaining ingredients and simmer 20–30 minutes while flavors meld. Taste and adjust seasonings, if needed.

Lentil Curry Soup {V}

Makes 4–6 *servings*

1¼ cups dried light-colored or red lentils, sorted and rinsed
1 bay leaf
6 cups water
2 tablespoons olive oil
1 small onion, chopped
1 tablespoon chopped green chile
1 clove garlic, minced
1 teaspoon finely minced fresh gingerroot
1 teaspoon turmeric
1 teaspoon cumin
½ teaspoon masala-blend spice
Pinch cayenne pepper
2 plum tomatoes, chopped
1 teaspoon lemon juice
Salt

In a large saucepan, bring lentils and bay leaf to a boil in water; reduce heat and simmer for about 1 hour, until lentils are very soft. Discard bay leaf.

Meanwhile, in a medium frying pan, heat oil and saute onion, chile, and garlic for 2–3 minutes, until onion begins to turn translucent. Add spices to the onion and saute 1–2 minutes more. Add tomatoes and lemon juice; cook until some of the tomato liquid evaporates. Add the onion and tomato mixture to the lentils and combine well. Season with salt.

NOTE: This soup is best when made a day ahead, refrigerated, and warmed before serving.

Lentil, Chick Pea, and Greens Soup {V}

Makes 4 servings

2 carrots, cut in pieces
1 medium onion,
    quartered
2 ribs celery, cut in
    pieces
1–2 cloves garlic, sliced
2 tablespoons olive oil
4 cups water
1 (14.5-ounce) can
    vegetable broth
1 cup dried lentils,
    sorted and rinsed
1 (15-ounce) can chick
    peas, drained and
    rinsed
1 (14.5-ounce) can
    stewed tomatoes
1 Knorr vegetable
    bouillon cube
1/4 teaspoon chile powder
4 cups chopped fresh
    cooking greens
    (spinach, kale, chard,
    mustard, etc.)
Salt and pepper

Pulse carrots, onion, celery, and garlic together in a food processor until very fine but not liquefied. In a large saucepan, saute the carrot mixture in oil for 2–3 minutes. Add all remaining ingredients except greens. Cover and bring to a low boil and cook for 30 minutes, or until lentils are soft. Add greens and boil soup another 2–4 minutes. Season to taste with salt and pepper.

Vegetable Soup with Lentils {V}

Makes 6 8 *servings*

1½ cups dried lentils

6 cups water

1 tablespoon vegetable-flavored bouillon granules

1 (15-ounce) can diced tomatoes, with liquid

2 tablespoons parsley flakes

1 large onion, diced

2 carrots, thinly sliced

4 medium potatoes, peeled and cubed

1 bay leaf

½ teaspoon salt

¼ teaspoon pepper

1 clove garlic, minced

Combine all ingredients in a large Dutch oven. Bring to a boil; cover, reduce heat, and simmer 1½–2 hours, stirring occasionally. Add more water as it cooks, if needed. Discard bay leaf.

White Hot Chili

Makes 4–6 *servings*

1 medium onion, thickly
    sliced and quartered
4 stalks celery, sliced
1–2 tablespoons
    vegetable oil
4 carrots, diced
3 cups chicken broth
1/4 teaspoon hot sauce
2 teaspoons lime juice
1 bay leaf
1/2 teaspoon dried
    cilantro or 1 small
    handful freshly
    chopped
1/2 teaspoon Season-All
1/4 teaspoon garlic
    powder
1 teaspoon salt
1 (4-ounce) can diced
    green chiles
2 (15-ounce) cans great
    Northern or other
    white beans
2 cups diced rotisserie
    chicken

In a medium soup pot, saute onion and celery in oil for about 5 minutes, until partly tender. Add carrots and saute for 2 minutes more.

Add all remaining ingredients, cover with a lid, and bring to boil. Let boil on medium-high for 3–5 minutes, and then reduce to simmer. Taste a spoonful (not just the liquid on the tip of a spoon, or you won't get the full flavor) for flavor base, heat, and saltiness. Adjust as desired. This soup tastes even better the next day.

VARIATION: If you like more heat, substitute a small can of jalapenos for the diced chiles.

Spicy Three-Bean Soup

Makes 12 servings

1 pound ground beef
1 teaspoon chili powder
1 teaspoon cumin
1/2 teaspoon cayenne
pepper
1/2 teaspoon garlic
powder
9 cups chicken broth
1 (14.5-ounce) can diced
tomatoes, with liquid
1 teaspoon red chile
pepper flakes or
black pepper
2 medium carrots,
chopped
2 leeks, cleaned and
sliced
1 cup dried pinto beans
1 cup dried navy beans
or great Northern
white beans
1 cup dried kidney
beans
Parmesan cheese

Cook hamburger in a large frying pan over medium-high heat until browned. Season with chili powder, cumin, cayenne pepper, and garlic powder. Spoon into a 6-quart slow cooker. Add broth, tomatoes, red pepper flakes, carrots, leeks, and beans. Cover and cook on low for 7–8 hours or on high for 4–5 hours. Make sure beans are tender. Serve with cheese.

Slow-Cooked Black Bean Soup {V}

Makes 6–8 *servings*

2 1/2 cups dried black beans, sorted and rinsed

1 generous cup chopped onion

3/4 cup chopped celery

2 cups chopped carrot

1 bay leaf

8–10 cups water, more if needed

3 Knorr vegetable bouillon cubes

1 tablespoon cumin

1 teaspoon oregano

1 teaspoon red chile flakes

Juice of 1 lime

1 avocado or prepared guacamole

Place all ingredients except avocado in a 4-quart slow cooker; cover then turn heat to high. Cook on high for 4–6 hours or on low for 8–10 hours, until beans are soft. If need be, turn cooker to high for a couple of hours at the end to finish cooking the beans—whatever combination suits your schedule. Don't worry about overcooking.

Before serving, discard bay leaf and puree the soup to a consistency you like using a hand-held blender or in an upright blender.* Garnish individual dishes of soup with diced avocado or a teaspoonful of guacamole.

*If the beans absorb all the water during cooking, add 2–3 cups more. There needs to be some amount of liquid for the blender to operate properly.

Sausage and Black Bean Soup

Makes 8 servings

6 strips bacon

2 cups dried black beans, sorted and rinsed

1 cup chopped onion

1 cup chopped celery

2 cups chopped carrot

8–10 cups water, more if needed

3 teaspoons beef base or 3 cubes beef bouillon

2 teaspoons cumin

1 teaspoon Creole seasoning

1 teaspoon dried basil

2 teaspoons red wine vinegar

1/2–1 pound andouille sausage, sliced

2 hardboiled eggs, chopped

Using a large frying pan, cook the bacon and drain all but 1 tablespoon of the fat. Transfer bacon and reserved fat to a large soup pot containing the beans. Add onion, celery, carrots, and water. Bring to a boil then reduce heat and continue at a low boil for 3–4 hours, stirring occasionally, until beans are soft. Once the beans have absorbed the water so you can't see it above the beans, add more water and bring to a boil again, then reduce heat.

When beans are nearly cooked, add the bouillon, seasonings, vinegar, and sausage for the last hour of cooking time. Garnish bowls of soup with chopped egg.

Shredded-Beef Chili

Makes 10–12 cups

1 (2-pound) cross rib
   roast, trimmed of fat
1 tablespoon vegetable
   oil
1 (1.3-ounce) packet
   onion soup and
   dip mix
1 (14.5-ounce) can beef
   broth
1 (14-ounce) can diced
   tomatoes
1 small onion, chopped
2 ribs celery, sliced
1/4 teaspoon garlic
   powder
1 teaspoon chili powder
1/2 teaspoon paprika
3 cups water, divided
2 (15-ounce) cans kidney
   or other red beans,
   drained and rinsed
1 (15-ounce) can black
   beans, drained and
   rinsed
1 (8-ounce) can tomato
   sauce

In a medium frying pan, brown the
beef roast in hot oil, both sides.
Transfer to a 3½-quart or larger
slow cooker. Sprinkle soup mix
over the roast then add the broth,
tomatoes, onion, celery, and spices.
Gently mix ingredients together,
covering the roast. Cover and cook
on low for 8–10 hours, until beef is
tender and all remaining beef fat
has liquefied. Add 1 cup water during the cooking time to replenish
evaporated liquid.

When beef is cooked, turn off
slow cooker and gently shred the
beef, using two forks. Add beans,
tomato sauce, and remaining water
and stir well. Replace the lid and
cook on high for about an hour
until the beans are well heated and
the flavors meld.

Smokin' Hot Chipotle Chili

Makes 10 servings

1 pound dried red beans,
   soaked overnight
8 cups water
2 pounds ground beef,
   browned
1 large onion, chopped
1 cup chopped celery
1 large green bell
   pepper, chopped
1/2 cup shredded carrot
2 tablespoons beef
   bouillon powder
1 (6-ounce) can tomato
   paste
2 (14.5-ounce) cans fire-
   roasted tomatoes
1 cup ketchup
3 chipotle chiles in
   adobo sauce, minced
1 teaspoon liquid smoke

Rinse soaked beans and place in a large soup pot with water. Bring to a boil and cook, covered, for 2 hours. When beans are soft, add all remaining ingredients and simmer for about 1 hour; chili will thicken while it cooks. Add more water if needed.

Smoky Sweet Chili

Makes 12–15 servings

1 pound bacon, cut in
small pieces
1 large onion, chopped
1 pound ground beef or
pork, browned
3 (15-ounce) cans pork
and beans
2 (15-ounce) cans
kidney beans,
drained and rinsed
2 (15-ounce) cans great
Northern beans,
drained and rinsed
1/2 cup chopped green
bell pepper, optional
1 cup ketchup
1/2 cup loosely packed
brown sugar
2 teaspoons liquid
smoke
3 tablespoons vinegar
1/2 teaspoon pepper

Brown bacon and onion together
in a large frying pan; drain and
discard fat. Place all ingredients
in a 6-quart slow cooker and mix
well. Cook on low for 5–8 hours.
Alternatively, bake in a large tightly
covered casserole or Dutch oven at
350 degrees for about 1½ hours.

Game Day Chili

Makes **12** *or more servings*

1 pound ground beef
1 pound ground pork
1 large onion, chopped
**1 (6-ounce) can tomato
    paste**
**3 (15-ounce) cans kidney
    beans, drained and
    rinsed**
**2 (15-ounce) cans black
    beans, drained and
    rinsed**
**1 (10-ounce) can
    original or mild
    Ro-Tel tomatoes with
    diced chiles**
**2 (8-ounce) cans tomato
    sauce**
**1 (14.5-ounce) can beef
    broth**
4 cups water
1 teaspoon chili powder
2 teaspoons salt
**Optional garnishes:
    sour cream, grated
    cheddar cheese,
    sliced green onions,
    jalapeno chiles**

In batches, brown the beef and pork with onion and tomato paste in a large frying pan; transfer to a large soup pot. Add all other ingredients except the garnishes. Cover and bring to a boil; reduce heat and simmer, stirring frequently, for 1–2 hours, while flavors meld. Serve with optional garnishes.

Simple Turkey Chili

Makes 4–6 servings

1½ teaspoons olive oil
1 pound ground turkey
1 onion, chopped
2 cups water
1 (28-ounce) can
   crushed tomatoes
1 (15-ounce) can kidney
   or black beans,
   drained and rinsed
1 tablespoon minced
   garlic
2 tablespoons chili
   powder
½ teaspoon paprika
½ teaspoon dried
   oregano
½ teaspoon cayenne
   pepper
½ teaspoon cumin
½ teaspoon salt
½ teaspoon pepper

Heat oil in a large soup pot over medium heat. Place turkey in the pot and cook until evenly brown. Stir in onion, and cook until tender.

Pour water into the pot. Mix in tomatoes, beans, and garlic. Add seasonings. Bring to a boil. Reduce heat to low, cover, and simmer for 30 minutes. If chili is too thick, add a little water.

NOTE: Recipe from my friend Keri, who says, "It's so healthy!"

Spicy-Sweet Pork and Pinto Chili

Makes 12 or more servings

1 pound dried pinto
  beans, sorted and
  rinsed
1½ cups chopped onion
1½ cups chopped celery
2 tablespoons chicken
  bouillon powder
6–8 cups water, divided
2 (4-ounce) cans diced
  green chiles
4–6 cups shredded
  cooked pork*
2 teaspoons Mexican
  oregano
2 teaspoons cumin
2 (14.5-ounce) cans
  diced tomatoes
1 cup honey barbecue
  sauce

In a large tightly covered saucepan or Dutch oven, lightly boil beans, onion, celery, and bouillon in 6 cups water until beans are tender, 2–2½ hours. Check water several times during cooking and add enough more so the beans are just covered. When beans are tender, add all remaining ingredients and mix well. Cook, covered, for 30–45 minutes more to meld flavors. Taste and adjust seasonings.

*Try a Boston butt, salted and roasted in a Dutch oven at 300 degrees for 3–4 hours, or purchase a tub of sweet pulled pork and reduce barbecue sauce to ¼ cup.

Three Sisters Soup

Makes 6–8 *servings*

1 medium onion, chopped
1 red bell pepper, finely
    chopped
2 tablespoons vegetable
    oil
1–2 cloves garlic, minced
1 (29-ounce) can
    pumpkin puree, or 4
    cups pureed winter
    squash (butternut,
    hubbard, banana)
2 cups water
2 Knorr chicken
    bouillon cubes or
    1 1/2 tablespoons
    bouillon powder
2 teaspoons cumin
1/2 teaspoon cayenne
    pepper
2 (14.5-ounce) cans
    beans (cut green,
    black, pinto), drained
    and rinsed
1 (14-ounce) bag frozen
    corn, thawed
2 cups half-and-half
1/2 bunch fresh cilantro,
    chopped

In a large saucepan, saute onion and bell pepper in oil for 3–4 minutes, until onion begins to turn translucent. Add garlic and saute 3 minutes more, stirring. Add pumpkin, water, bouillon, and spices and mix well. Cover and bring to a boil, stirring frequently; reduce heat and simmer for 8–10 minutes. Add beans and corn and simmer 5 minutes, stirring. Stir in half-and-half and cilantro and heat through.

Split Pea with Ham Soup

Makes 8–10 *servings*

1 pound dried split peas
1 bay leaf
1 medium onion, chopped
2 ribs celery, chopped
1 cup grated carrot
6 cups water
2 teaspoons chicken
   bouillon powder or
   ham base
2 cups diced cooked ham
1/4 teaspoon pepper

In a large covered saucepan, bring peas, bay leaf, vegetables, and water to a boil. Reduce heat to a low boil until peas break down and thicken the liquid, about 1 1/2 hours. Stir frequently to prevent sticking. Remove bay leaf and puree soup, if desired. Return to heat and add bouillon, ham, and pepper. Simmer for 30 minutes, stirring frequently. Thin soup with more water, if needed. Taste and adjust seasonings.

Rosemary Split Pea Soup

Makes 8–10 *servings*

1 pound dried split peas,
   green and yellow mix
1 medium onion, chopped
1 sprig fresh rosemary
6 cups water
3 medium potatoes, cut
   in small cubes
2 cups chopped carrots
2 ribs celery, chopped
3 cups diced cooked ham
1 tablespoon chicken
   bouillon powder
1/4 teaspoon pepper

In a large covered saucepan, bring peas, onion, and rosemary to a boil in water. Reduce heat to a low boil until peas are tender, about 1 1/2 hours. Remove rosemary and smash the peas with a potato masher. In a separate large saucepan, cook all remaining ingredients in enough water to just cover, until vegetables are tender. Add vegetables and meat to the peas, with as much of the cooking liquid as you like, and mix well. Simmer soup for about 30 minutes.

Vegetarian Chili {V}

Makes 8–10 servings

4 tablespoons olive oil
1 medium onion, chopped
2 cloves garlic, minced
1 cup chopped carrot
3/4 cup chopped celery
1/2 cup chopped green or
   red bell pepper
4 (14.5-ounce) cans
   beans (1 can each
   kidney, black, pinto,
   red), drained and
   rinsed
2 (10-ounce) cans diced
   tomatoes with chiles
2 (14.5-ounce) cans
   diced tomatoes
2 (14.5-ounce) cans
   corn, drained
2 teaspoons cumin
1 teaspoon chili powder
1 1/2 teaspoons dried
   epazote
1 teaspoon Mexican
   oregano
2 teaspoons salt
1 teaspoon liquid smoke
Optional garnishes:
   sour cream, grated
   cheese, sliced green
   onions, corn chips

In a large soup pot, heat oil over medium-high heat until it's shimmery. Add onion, garlic, carrot and celery to the pot and stir to coat with oil. Saute 8–10 minutes, stirring frequently.

Add all remaining ingredients. Cover the pot and bring to a boil; reduce heat and simmer for 30–45 minutes, stirring occasionally. Add a cup of water, if needed, during cooking. Serve with garnishes, if desired.

Black-Eyed Peas, Turnips, and Greens Soup

Makes 4–6 servings

1½ cups dried black-eyed peas, sorted, rinsed and presoaked per package directions
1 medium onion, chopped
1 piece salt pork*
2 teaspoons bacon grease
6 cups water
3 beef bouillon cubes
2 (1-pound) packages frozen turnips and greens
Salt and pepper

Place the soaked beans in a large soup pot with onion, pork, bacon grease, and water. Cover and bring to a boil; reduce to a low boil for about 2 hours, or until beans are tender. Add the bouillon and frozen vegetables (can be thawed but not necessary). Simmer about 30 minutes, until vegetables are tender and heated through. Adjust seasonings with salt and pepper.

*You can omit the salt pork and instead add 1½ cups chopped deli ham when you add the turnips.

NOTE: On the stove, this recipe takes about 3 hours to cook. In a slow cooker on low, the beans will soften in about 6 hours.

Soups from
the Pantry

Southwestern Pantry Soup

Makes 6–8 *servings*

2 1/2 cups water
1 (7.25-ounce) box
    macaroni and cheese
1 teaspoon butter
1 (15-ounce) can chili
    with beans
1 (14.5-ounce) can diced
    tomatoes
1 teaspoons beef bouillon
2–3 tablespoons salsa,
    optional
1 1/2 cups milk, divided
Corn chips

In a 4-quart saucepan, heat the water to boiling then add macaroni. Boil lightly for 5 minutes, stirring frequently to prevent sticking. Add cheese packet and stir. Add chili, tomatoes, bouillon, and salsa, if using. Stir to mix well and heat through. Add milk 1/2 cup at a time until soup is a consistency you like. Serve with corn chips for garnish.

Spinach and Lentil Fusion Soup

Makes 4 *servings*

1 cup frozen southern-
    style hash browns
1 teaspoon dehydrated
    onion flakes
1 teaspoon chicken
    bouillon powder
1 cup water
1 (10-ounce) box frozen
    chopped spinach

1/4 teaspoon seasoned salt
2 (19-ounce) cans lentil
    soup

In a covered medium saucepan, bring potatoes, onion, and bouillon to a boil in water. Meanwhile, heat spinach in microwave and drain excess water. Add spinach, salt, and canned soup to the pan. Stir and heat together. Taste and adjust seasonings.

Cheesy Tuna Pasta Soup

Makes 4–6 servings

1 (7.25-ounce) box macaroni and cheese
1 tablespoon butter
2 tablespoons flour
1/2 teaspoon Season-All
4 teaspoons chicken bouillon powder
1/4 teaspoon dill weed
3 cups milk
1 (15-ounce) can peas and carrots, drained
1 (5-ounce) can chunk light tuna in water
Pepper

Cook macaroni according to package directions; drain. Return to saucepan with butter, contents of cheese flavoring packet, flour, Season-All, bouillon, and dill. Mix together then add all remaining ingredients. On medium-high, heat soup without boiling, stirring frequently.

Helper Taco Soup

Makes 6–8 *cups*

3 cups water
1 pound ground beef,
    browned
1 tablespoon dehydrated
    onion flakes
1 box Double Cheesy
    Quesadilla
    Hamburger Helper
1 (14.5-ounce) can diced
    tomatoes
2½ teaspoons beef base
1 (14.5-ounce) can
    kidney beans,
    drained and rinsed
1 (14.5-ounce) can corn,
    drained
Pepper
Corn chips

In a medium saucepan, bring water to a boil. Add ground beef, onion, and contents of both the rice and sauce packets from the Hamburger Helper. Cover and simmer for about 20 minutes, until the rice grains swell and are no longer crunchy. Add all remaining ingredients except the corn chips, and bring to a low boil. Cook, stirring occasionally, for about 10 minutes while ingredients heat. Serve with chips.

Easy Taco Soup

Makes 6 servings

2 (14.5-ounce) cans chili
1 (14.5-ounce) can black
   beans, drained and
   rinsed
1 (14.5-ounce) can corn,
   drained
1 (2.25-ounce) can
   sliced black olives
1 (14.5-ounce) can
   diced Italian-style
   tomatoes
1 (14.5-ounce) can beef
   broth
Sour cream
Sliced green onions
Grated cheddar cheese
Corn chips

In a medium-size soup pot, mix together all ingredients except sour cream, onions, cheese, and corn chips and heat over medium-high until lightly boiling. Ladle into bowls and garnish as desired.

Cheesy Potato Soup

Makes 4 servings

1 (4-ounce) pouch
instant butter-flavor
mashed potatoes
1 (14.5-ounce) can
chicken broth
3 cups milk, divided
1/4 teaspoon marjoram
2 tablespoons bacon bits
3/4 cup grated cheddar
cheese
1 green onion, thinly
sliced

In a large microwave-safe bowl, mix potatoes into broth and microwave on high for 2 minutes and then stir. Fold 1 1/2 cups milk into potatoes and cook for 1 more minute. Add remaining milk and other ingredients, mix well, and microwave until hot, pausing to stir every minute.

Easiest Clam Chowder

Makes 4 servings

2 (10.5-ounce) cans
cream of potato soup,
condensed
1 (10.5-ounce) can
cream of celery soup,
condensed
2 cups milk
1 (6.5-ounce) can minced
clams, with juice
1/2 teaspoon Old Bay
seasoning
Oyster crackers

Heat soups and milk together in a medium saucepan, stirring frequently, just until the soup begins to boil. Add clams and seasoning, and let simmer for 3–4 minutes. Serve with crackers on top.

Ravin' Ramen with Shrimp Soup

Makes 4 servings

2 (12-ounce) packages
   fresh vegetables
   (carrot and snap pea)
2 packets Oriental-
   flavored ramen
   noodles
1/8 teaspoon Cajun
   seasoning
2 pinches chicken
   bouillon powder
Pepper

1 (6-ounce) can
   deveined shrimp
   or 1/4 pound cooked
   small shrimp

Steam vegetables in the microwave for 2–3 minutes, until tender.

Cook ramen noodles according to package directions; stir in the flavor packets and other seasonings. Combine vegetables and shrimp with the soup and serve.

Chicken Vegetable Ramen Soup

Makes 4 servings

2 (12-ounce) packages
   frozen mixed
   vegetables
2 packets ramen noodles,
   chicken or vegetable-
   chicken flavor
1/8 teaspoon dill weed
Pepper
1 (6-ounce) can white
   meat chicken

Steam vegetables in the microwave about 3 minutes, until tender.

Cook ramen noodles according to package directions; stir in the flavor packets and other seasonings. Combine vegetables and chicken with the soup. Heat and serve.

Cream of Dilly Green Bean Soup

Makes 4 servings

2 (14.5-ounce) cans
   green beans, drained
1 (10.5-ounce) can
   cream of chicken
   soup, condensed
1 (10.5-ounce) can
   cream of celery soup,
   condensed
2 cups milk
1 tablespoon butter
$^1/_2$ teaspoon dill weed
Grated cheese, of choice

Puree the beans and soups together in two batches. Place all ingredients in a medium saucepan and thoroughly heat. Serve with cheese for garnish.

Creamy Broccoli with Chicken Soup

Makes 4 servings

2 (14.5-ounce) cans cream of chicken soup, condensed
1 (12-ounce) can evaporated milk
³/₄ cup water
1 (6-ounce) can chicken, drained and broken up
2 cups frozen chopped broccoli

Place canned soup and milk in a medium saucepan and heat over medium heat, stirring frequently. Let come to a low boil then reduce to simmer and stir until well blended. Add remaining ingredients and thoroughly heat.

Simple Chicken-Vegetable Soup

Makes 4 servings

2 (14.5-ounce) cans Veg-All, with liquid
1 (14.5-ounce) can cream-style corn
2 small chicken bouillon cubes
1 (6-ounce) can chicken, broken apart
1 cup water
Salt and pepper

Mix all ingredients in a medium saucepan. Cover and bring to a boil on medium heat. Reduce to simmer for 5–10 minutes. Adjust seasonings.

Sweet Pumpkin Soup

Makes 6 servings

1 (29-ounce) can
  pumpkin
1 (14.5-ounce) can
  applesauce
1 (14.5-ounce) can
  chicken broth
1 teaspoon chicken
  bouillon powder
1/2 teaspoon salt
1/4 teaspoon cinnamon
1/8 teaspoon ginger
1/8 teaspoon allspice

1/3 cup pancake syrup
1 (12-ounce) can
  evaporated milk
Graham crackers

In a large saucepan, heat pumpkin, applesauce, and broth together. Whisk to combine. Whisk bouillon and spices into syrup then add syrup and milk to soup. Stir well and bring just to boiling. Remove from heat. Garnish each bowl with crushed graham crackers, if desired.

Tomato-Corn Curry Soup {V}

Makes 4 servings

1 (14.5-ounce) can
  cream-style corn
1 (10.5-ounce) can
  tomato soup,
  condensed
1 (12-ounce) can
  evaporated milk
1/8 teaspoon onion salt
1/2–1 teaspoon curry
  powder

1 cup shelled edamame
Sour cream, optional

Puree the corn. In a medium saucepan over medium heat, combine all ingredients. Heat just until the soup starts to boil, then reduce heat to simmer for 2 minutes. Serve with a dollop of sour cream, if desired.

Easy Chicken Gumbo

Makes 4–6 *servings*

1 (14.5-ounce) can
   chicken broth
1 (14.5-ounce) can
   Italian-style diced
   tomatoes, drained
1 (14.5-ounce) can diced
   carrots
1 (10-ounce) package
   frozen okra, sliced
1 (5-ounce) can chicken
¾ cup instant rice
2 small chicken bouillon
   cubes

2 teaspoons dehydrated
   onion flakes
1 teaspoon parsley
⅛ teaspoon garlic salt
Dash hot sauce
Salt
2 cups water

Place all ingredients in a medium saucepan and bring to a boil over medium-high heat. Reduce heat and simmer for 5 minutes. Turn off heat and let sit for 5 minutes before serving. Taste and adjust seasonings.

Smokie O's Soup

Makes 4–6 *servings*

1 (14-ounce) package
   Lit'l Smokies, cut
   bite-size
2 (14.5-ounce) cans
   SpaghettiOs
1 (14.5-ounce) can pork
   and beans
1 (14.5-ounce) can
   French-cut green
   beans, drained
1 (10.5-ounce) can
   tomato soup,
   condensed

1 cup water
¼ cup smoky barbecue
   sauce
1 tablespoon prepared
   mustard

Mix all ingredients together in a medium-size saucepan and bring to a simmer over medium heat for about 20 minutes, stirring frequently, until sausages are heated through.

Gypsy Stew

Makes 6 servings

1 (14.5-ounce) can
  chicken broth
1 (15-ounce) can lima
  beans, drained
1 (14.5-ounce) can peas
  and carrots, drained
1 cup cut-up cooked
  chicken
4 breakfast sausage
  links, cooked and
  sliced
1 teaspoon paprika
1 (.87-ounce) packet
  chicken gravy mix
1 (14.5-ounce) can
  yams, drained and
  cut bite-size
Salt and pepper

In a large saucepan, heat the broth, beans, peas and carrots, chicken, sausage, and paprika. Cover and bring to a low boil over medium heat, stirring frequently. When the liquid begins to bubble, stir in contents of the gravy packet and let boil for 2 minutes. Gently fold in yams, cover pan, and let simmer for 4–5 minutes, until yams are heated. The stew should be thick. Adjust seasoning with salt and pepper.

Beefy Mushroom and Rice Soup

Makes 4–6 *servings*

1 (6.8-ounce) box beef-flavored Rice-A-Roni
2 (14.5-ounce) cans chicken broth
1/2 cup ketchup
2 (4-ounce) cans mushroom stems and pieces, drained
1 (14-ounce) can carrots, drained
1 (15-ounce) can white beans, drained and rinsed
1 (13-ounce) can evaporated milk
1/2 cup milk

In a medium saucepan, cook Rice-A-Roni on the stovetop according to package directions, except substitute chicken broth for most of the water; add enough water to make 2¼ cups total liquid. When rice is tender, stir in ketchup; then add mushrooms, carrots, beans, and milks; mix together well. Stirring frequently, bring to a simmer for 2–3 minutes to thoroughly heat.

Index {V} indicates vegetarian